50 Flavors of the Mediterranean Recipes for Home

By: Kelly Johnson

Table of Contents

- Mediterranean Grilled Vegetable Salad
- Lemon Garlic Roasted Chicken
- Greek Style Lamb Kebabs
- Mediterranean Pasta with Sun-Dried Tomatoes and Olives
- Spanakopita (Greek Spinach Pie)
- Moroccan Tagine with Couscous
- Italian Caprese Salad
- Hummus with Pita Bread
- Greek Moussaka
- Ratatouille (French Provençal Vegetable Stew)
- Shakshuka (North African Tomato and Egg Dish)
- Tzatziki (Greek Yogurt and Cucumber Dip)
- Italian Margherita Pizza
- Falafel with Tahini Sauce
- Greek Feta and Olive Tart
- Mediterranean Stuffed Peppers
- Italian Minestrone Soup
- Greek Lemon Potatoes
- Moroccan Chicken Tagine with Preserved Lemons
- Caponata (Sicilian Eggplant Dish)
- Greek Souvlaki with Tzatziki Sauce
- Mediterranean Baked Fish with Herbs and Lemon
- Italian Risotto with Seafood
- Turkish Baklava
- Mediterranean Chickpea Salad
- Greek Lemon Chicken Souvlaki
- Italian Bruschetta with Tomato and Basil
- Moroccan Lamb Tagine with Apricots and Almonds
- Mediterranean Grilled Shrimp with Garlic and Herbs
- Spanakopita Stuffed Chicken Breast
- Italian Eggplant Parmesan
- Lebanese Fattoush Salad
- Greek Spanakopita Dip
- Moroccan Chickpea and Vegetable Tagine
- Mediterranean Baked Eggplant with Tomatoes and Feta

- Italian Gnocchi with Pesto Sauce
- Greek Orzo Salad with Feta and Olives
- Moroccan Spiced Couscous with Roasted Vegetables
- Mediterranean Grilled Lamb Chops with Mint Sauce
- Italian Panzanella Salad with Tomatoes and Bread
- Greek Tzatziki Pasta Salad
- Moroccan Harira Soup
- Mediterranean Stuffed Zucchini Boats
- Italian Sausage and Pepper Pasta
- Greek Spinach and Feta Stuffed Chicken Breast
- Moroccan Chicken Pastilla (Pie)
- Mediterranean Roasted Red Pepper Hummus
- Italian Cannellini Bean Soup with Rosemary
- Greek Lemon Garlic Roasted Potatoes
- Moroccan Orange and Olive Salad

Mediterranean Grilled Vegetable Salad

Ingredients:

- 1 medium eggplant, sliced into rounds
- 1 medium zucchini, sliced lengthwise
- 1 red bell pepper, seeded and quartered
- 1 yellow bell pepper, seeded and quartered
- 1 red onion, sliced into rounds
- 1 cup cherry tomatoes
- 1/4 cup extra virgin olive oil
- 2 tablespoons balsamic vinegar
- 2 cloves garlic, minced
- 1 teaspoon dried oregano
- Salt and black pepper to taste
- Fresh basil leaves for garnish

Instructions:

1. Preheat your grill to medium-high heat.
2. In a small bowl, whisk together the olive oil, balsamic vinegar, minced garlic, dried oregano, salt, and black pepper to make the marinade.
3. Place the sliced eggplant, zucchini, bell peppers, and onion in a large bowl. Pour the marinade over the vegetables and toss until evenly coated.
4. Place the marinated vegetables on the preheated grill. Cook for about 4-5 minutes on each side, or until they are tender and have grill marks.
5. While the vegetables are grilling, you can also grill the cherry tomatoes on a skewer for about 2-3 minutes, just until they begin to soften.
6. Once the vegetables are grilled to your liking, remove them from the grill and let them cool slightly.
7. Arrange the grilled vegetables on a serving platter or salad bowl. Sprinkle with fresh basil leaves for garnish.
8. Serve the Mediterranean Grilled Vegetable Salad warm or at room temperature. You can also drizzle some extra olive oil or balsamic vinegar on top if desired.

Enjoy your delicious and healthy Mediterranean Grilled Vegetable Salad!

Lemon Garlic Roasted Chicken

Ingredients:

- 1 whole chicken (about 3-4 pounds)
- 4 cloves garlic, minced
- Zest of 1 lemon
- Juice of 1 lemon
- 2 tablespoons olive oil
- 1 tablespoon fresh thyme leaves (or 1 teaspoon dried thyme)
- 1 teaspoon paprika
- Salt and pepper to taste
- 1 lemon, thinly sliced
- Fresh parsley for garnish (optional)

Instructions:

1. Preheat your oven to 375°F (190°C).
2. Rinse the chicken under cold water and pat dry with paper towels. Place the chicken in a roasting pan or baking dish.
3. In a small bowl, mix together the minced garlic, lemon zest, lemon juice, olive oil, thyme, paprika, salt, and pepper to make the marinade.
4. Rub the marinade all over the chicken, making sure to coat it evenly, including under the skin if possible.
5. Stuff the cavity of the chicken with the lemon slices.
6. Tie the legs together with kitchen twine if desired to help the chicken cook evenly.
7. Place the chicken in the preheated oven and roast for about 1 hour and 15 minutes to 1 hour and 30 minutes, or until the internal temperature reaches 165°F (75°C) when tested with a meat thermometer.
8. Halfway through cooking, baste the chicken with the pan juices to keep it moist.
9. Once the chicken is cooked through and golden brown, remove it from the oven and let it rest for about 10 minutes before carving.
10. Garnish the roasted chicken with fresh parsley if desired, and serve with your favorite side dishes.

Enjoy your flavorful Lemon Garlic Roasted Chicken!

Greek Style Lamb Kebabs

Ingredients:

- 1 lb (450g) lamb leg or shoulder, cut into 1-inch cubes
- 1 red onion, cut into chunks
- 1 red bell pepper, cut into chunks
- 1 yellow bell pepper, cut into chunks
- 1 zucchini, sliced
- 8-10 cherry tomatoes
- Wooden or metal skewers (if using wooden skewers, soak them in water for at least 30 minutes before grilling)

For the Marinade:

- 1/4 cup extra virgin olive oil
- Juice of 1 lemon
- 3 cloves garlic, minced
- 2 teaspoons dried oregano
- 1 teaspoon dried thyme
- 1 teaspoon dried rosemary
- Salt and black pepper to taste

For Serving (Optional):

- Tzatziki sauce
- Lemon wedges
- Fresh parsley, chopped

Instructions:

1. In a bowl, mix together the ingredients for the marinade: olive oil, lemon juice, minced garlic, dried oregano, dried thyme, dried rosemary, salt, and black pepper.
2. Place the cubed lamb in a shallow dish or resealable plastic bag. Pour the marinade over the lamb and toss until the meat is evenly coated. Cover the dish or seal the bag, then refrigerate for at least 1 hour, or ideally overnight, to marinate.
3. Preheat your grill to medium-high heat.

4. Thread the marinated lamb cubes onto skewers, alternating with pieces of onion, bell pepper, zucchini, and cherry tomatoes.
5. Brush the vegetables with a little extra olive oil to prevent them from sticking to the grill.
6. Place the kebabs on the preheated grill and cook for about 8-10 minutes, turning occasionally, or until the lamb is cooked to your desired level of doneness and the vegetables are tender and slightly charred.
7. Once the kebabs are cooked, remove them from the grill and let them rest for a few minutes.
8. Serve the Greek Style Lamb Kebabs hot with tzatziki sauce, lemon wedges, and chopped fresh parsley on the side, if desired.

Enjoy these flavorful and juicy Greek Style Lamb Kebabs!

Mediterranean Pasta with Sun-Dried Tomatoes and Olives

Ingredients:

- 8 oz (225g) pasta of your choice (such as penne, fusilli, or farfalle)
- 1/2 cup sun-dried tomatoes, drained and chopped
- 1/2 cup pitted Kalamata olives, sliced
- 2 tablespoons extra virgin olive oil
- 3 cloves garlic, minced
- 1/4 teaspoon red pepper flakes (optional)
- 1/4 cup fresh basil leaves, chopped
- 1/4 cup fresh parsley, chopped
- Salt and black pepper to taste
- Grated Parmesan cheese for serving (optional)

Instructions:

1. Cook the pasta according to the package instructions until al dente. Drain the cooked pasta, reserving about 1/4 cup of the pasta cooking water.
2. While the pasta is cooking, heat the olive oil in a large skillet over medium heat. Add the minced garlic and red pepper flakes (if using) and sauté for 1-2 minutes, or until the garlic is fragrant and lightly golden.
3. Add the chopped sun-dried tomatoes and sliced olives to the skillet. Cook for another 2-3 minutes, stirring occasionally.
4. Add the cooked pasta to the skillet, along with the reserved pasta cooking water. Toss everything together until the pasta is well coated with the sauce.
5. Stir in the chopped fresh basil and parsley, then season with salt and black pepper to taste. Cook for another minute to heat everything through.
6. Remove the skillet from the heat and transfer the Mediterranean Pasta with Sun-Dried Tomatoes and Olives to serving plates or a large bowl.
7. Serve the pasta hot, garnished with grated Parmesan cheese if desired.

Enjoy this flavorful and satisfying Mediterranean-inspired pasta dish!

Spanakopita (Greek Spinach Pie)

Ingredients:

- 1 pound (450g) fresh spinach, washed and chopped (or you can use frozen spinach, thawed and drained)
- 1/2 cup fresh parsley, chopped
- 1/2 cup fresh dill, chopped
- 1/2 cup green onions, chopped
- 1 cup crumbled feta cheese
- 1/4 cup grated Parmesan cheese
- 4 eggs, lightly beaten
- Salt and pepper to taste
- 1/4 teaspoon ground nutmeg
- 1/4 cup olive oil
- 1 package phyllo dough (about 16 sheets), thawed if frozen
- 1/2 cup unsalted butter, melted

Instructions:

1. Preheat your oven to 350°F (175°C). Lightly grease a 9x13 inch baking dish.
2. In a large bowl, combine the chopped spinach, parsley, dill, green onions, feta cheese, Parmesan cheese, beaten eggs, salt, pepper, and ground nutmeg. Mix well to combine.
3. In a separate small saucepan, heat the olive oil over medium heat.
4. Place one sheet of phyllo dough in the prepared baking dish and brush it lightly with melted butter. Repeat with 7 more sheets of phyllo dough, brushing each sheet with melted butter.
5. Spread the spinach and cheese mixture evenly over the layered phyllo dough in the baking dish.
6. Layer the remaining sheets of phyllo dough on top of the spinach mixture, brushing each sheet lightly with melted butter.
7. Use a sharp knife to score the top layer of phyllo dough into squares or triangles, being careful not to cut all the way through to the filling.
8. Bake the Spanakopita in the preheated oven for 45-50 minutes, or until the phyllo dough is golden brown and crispy.
9. Remove the Spanakopita from the oven and let it cool for a few minutes before slicing and serving.

10. Serve the Spanakopita warm or at room temperature. It's delicious as a main dish or as part of a Greek mezze spread.

Enjoy your homemade Spanakopita!

Moroccan Tagine with Couscous

Ingredients:

For the Tagine:

- 1 lb (450g) boneless chicken thighs, cut into chunks (you can also use lamb or beef)
- 2 tablespoons olive oil
- 1 onion, finely chopped
- 2 cloves garlic, minced
- 1 teaspoon ground cumin
- 1 teaspoon ground coriander
- 1 teaspoon ground cinnamon
- 1/2 teaspoon ground ginger
- 1/4 teaspoon ground turmeric
- 1/4 teaspoon cayenne pepper (optional, for heat)
- 1 can (14 oz/400g) diced tomatoes
- 1 cup chicken broth
- 1 cup carrots, sliced
- 1 cup potatoes, diced
- 1 cup green beans, trimmed and halved
- 1/2 cup dried apricots, chopped
- 1/4 cup sliced almonds, toasted (for garnish)
- Fresh cilantro or parsley, chopped (for garnish)
- Salt and black pepper to taste

For the Couscous:

- 1 cup couscous
- 1 cup chicken broth or water
- 1 tablespoon olive oil
- Salt to taste

Instructions:

For the Tagine:

1. Heat the olive oil in a large tagine or Dutch oven over medium heat. Add the chopped onion and cook until softened, about 5 minutes.
2. Add the minced garlic and cook for another minute, until fragrant.
3. Add the chicken pieces to the tagine and brown on all sides, about 5 minutes.
4. Stir in the ground cumin, ground coriander, ground cinnamon, ground ginger, ground turmeric, and cayenne pepper (if using). Cook for 1-2 minutes until the spices are fragrant.
5. Pour in the diced tomatoes and chicken broth. Stir to combine.
6. Add the sliced carrots, diced potatoes, halved green beans, and chopped dried apricots to the tagine. Season with salt and black pepper to taste.
7. Cover the tagine and simmer over low heat for about 30-40 minutes, or until the chicken is cooked through and the vegetables are tender.
8. While the tagine is cooking, prepare the couscous.

For the Couscous:

1. In a saucepan, bring the chicken broth or water to a boil.
2. Stir in the couscous, olive oil, and salt. Remove from heat, cover, and let it sit for 5 minutes.
3. Fluff the couscous with a fork to separate the grains.

To Serve:

1. Spoon the cooked couscous onto serving plates or a large platter.
2. Ladle the Moroccan Tagine over the couscous.
3. Garnish with toasted sliced almonds and chopped fresh cilantro or parsley.
4. Serve hot and enjoy the flavors of Morocco!

Feel free to adjust the ingredients or spices according to your taste preferences. Enjoy your Moroccan Tagine with Couscous!

Italian Caprese Salad

Ingredients:

- 4 ripe tomatoes, sliced
- 8 oz (225g) fresh mozzarella cheese, sliced
- 1/4 cup fresh basil leaves
- Extra virgin olive oil, for drizzling
- Balsamic glaze (optional), for drizzling
- Salt and black pepper to taste

Instructions:

1. Arrange the sliced tomatoes and mozzarella cheese alternately on a serving platter or individual plates, overlapping slightly.
2. Tuck fresh basil leaves between the slices of tomatoes and cheese.
3. Drizzle extra virgin olive oil over the tomato and mozzarella slices.
4. If desired, drizzle balsamic glaze over the salad for added sweetness and flavor.
5. Season the Caprese Salad with salt and black pepper to taste.
6. Serve immediately as a refreshing appetizer or side dish.

Caprese Salad is best enjoyed fresh, so try to serve it soon after assembling to preserve the flavors and textures of the ingredients. It's a simple yet elegant dish that showcases the delicious combination of ripe tomatoes, creamy mozzarella, and fragrant basil. Buon appetito!

Hummus with Pita Bread

Ingredients:

- 1 can (15 oz/425g) chickpeas (garbanzo beans), drained and rinsed
- 1/4 cup tahini (sesame paste)
- 2 cloves garlic, minced
- 3 tablespoons lemon juice
- 2 tablespoons extra virgin olive oil
- 1/2 teaspoon ground cumin
- Salt to taste
- Water (as needed for desired consistency)
- Optional toppings: extra olive oil, paprika, chopped parsley, toasted pine nuts

Instructions:

1. In a food processor, combine the chickpeas, tahini, minced garlic, lemon juice, olive oil, ground cumin, and a pinch of salt.
2. Process the mixture until smooth and creamy, scraping down the sides of the bowl as needed. If the hummus is too thick, you can add water, a tablespoon at a time, until you reach your desired consistency.
3. Taste the hummus and adjust the seasoning, adding more salt or lemon juice if needed.
4. Transfer the hummus to a serving bowl and drizzle with extra virgin olive oil. Sprinkle with paprika, chopped parsley, and toasted pine nuts, if desired, for extra flavor and presentation.
5. Serve the hummus with fresh pita bread for dipping.

Pita Bread:

Ingredients:

- 2 cups all-purpose flour
- 1 teaspoon salt
- 1 teaspoon sugar
- 2 teaspoons active dry yeast
- 1 cup warm water
- 1 tablespoon olive oil

Instructions:

1. In a large mixing bowl, combine the flour, salt, sugar, and yeast.
2. Gradually add the warm water and olive oil to the dry ingredients, stirring until a dough forms.
3. Knead the dough on a lightly floured surface for about 5-7 minutes, or until it becomes smooth and elastic.
4. Place the dough in a lightly oiled bowl, cover with a clean kitchen towel, and let it rise in a warm place for about 1-1.5 hours, or until doubled in size.
5. Preheat your oven to 450°F (230°C). If you have a baking stone, place it in the oven to preheat as well.
6. Punch down the risen dough and divide it into 6-8 equal-sized balls.
7. Roll out each ball of dough into a circle, about 1/4 inch thick.
8. Place the rolled-out dough circles onto a baking sheet or directly onto the preheated baking stone.
9. Bake the pita bread in the preheated oven for 5-7 minutes, or until puffed up and lightly golden brown.
10. Remove the pita bread from the oven and let them cool slightly before serving.

Serve the freshly baked pita bread alongside the homemade hummus for a delicious and satisfying snack or appetizer. Enjoy!

Greek Moussaka

Ingredients:

For the Moussaka:

- 2 large eggplants, sliced lengthwise into 1/4-inch thick slices
- Salt
- Olive oil for brushing
- 1 large onion, finely chopped
- 3 cloves garlic, minced
- 1 lb (450g) ground lamb or beef
- 1 can (14 oz/400g) diced tomatoes
- 2 tablespoons tomato paste
- 1 teaspoon dried oregano
- 1/2 teaspoon ground cinnamon
- Salt and black pepper to taste
- 1/2 cup dry red wine (optional)
- 1/4 cup chopped fresh parsley
- Grated Parmesan cheese for sprinkling (optional)

For the Béchamel Sauce:

- 4 tablespoons unsalted butter
- 1/4 cup all-purpose flour
- 2 cups whole milk
- 1/4 teaspoon ground nutmeg
- Salt and black pepper to taste
- 2 large eggs
- 1/2 cup grated Parmesan cheese

Instructions:

1. Preheat your oven to 400°F (200°C).
2. Place the sliced eggplant on a baking sheet lined with paper towels. Sprinkle both sides of the eggplant slices with salt and let them sit for about 15-20 minutes to release excess moisture. Pat the eggplant slices dry with paper towels.

3. Brush both sides of the eggplant slices with olive oil and arrange them in a single layer on baking sheets. Roast in the preheated oven for about 20-25 minutes, flipping halfway through, or until the eggplant is tender and lightly browned. Remove from the oven and set aside.
4. In a large skillet, heat some olive oil over medium heat. Add the chopped onion and minced garlic, and sauté until softened and fragrant, about 5 minutes.
5. Add the ground lamb or beef to the skillet, breaking it up with a spoon, and cook until browned and cooked through.
6. Stir in the diced tomatoes, tomato paste, dried oregano, ground cinnamon, salt, and black pepper. If using, add the red wine. Simmer for about 10-15 minutes, or until the sauce has thickened slightly. Remove from heat and stir in the chopped parsley. Set aside.
7. To make the béchamel sauce, melt the butter in a saucepan over medium heat. Stir in the flour and cook for 1-2 minutes, stirring constantly, until the mixture is smooth and bubbly.
8. Gradually whisk in the milk, stirring constantly to prevent lumps from forming. Cook until the sauce thickens and coats the back of a spoon, about 5-7 minutes.
9. Remove the saucepan from the heat and stir in the ground nutmeg, salt, and black pepper. Allow the sauce to cool slightly.
10. In a small bowl, lightly beat the eggs. Gradually whisk the beaten eggs into the warm béchamel sauce until well combined. Stir in the grated Parmesan cheese.
11. To assemble the moussaka, spread half of the roasted eggplant slices in the bottom of a greased 9x13 inch baking dish.
12. Spoon the meat mixture evenly over the eggplant layer.
13. Top the meat mixture with the remaining roasted eggplant slices.
14. Pour the béchamel sauce evenly over the top of the moussaka, spreading it out with a spatula to cover the entire surface.
15. Sprinkle the grated Parmesan cheese over the top of the moussaka, if desired.
16. Bake the moussaka in the preheated oven for about 45-50 minutes, or until the top is golden brown and bubbly.
17. Remove the moussaka from the oven and let it cool for a few minutes before slicing and serving.
18. Serve the moussaka warm, garnished with additional chopped parsley if desired.

Enjoy this delicious and comforting Greek Moussaka!

Ratatouille (French Provençal Vegetable Stew)

Ingredients:

- 1 large eggplant, diced
- 2 zucchinis, diced
- 2 bell peppers (red, yellow, or orange), diced
- 2 tomatoes, diced
- 1 onion, diced
- 3 cloves garlic, minced
- 2 tablespoons tomato paste
- 2 tablespoons olive oil
- 1 teaspoon dried thyme
- 1 teaspoon dried rosemary
- 1 teaspoon dried oregano
- Salt and black pepper to taste
- Fresh basil leaves, chopped, for garnish

Instructions:

1. Heat the olive oil in a large skillet or Dutch oven over medium heat.
2. Add the diced onion to the skillet and sauté until translucent, about 5 minutes.
3. Add the minced garlic to the skillet and cook for another minute, until fragrant.
4. Add the diced eggplant to the skillet and cook for about 5-7 minutes, stirring occasionally, until softened.
5. Stir in the diced zucchini, bell peppers, and tomatoes.
6. Add the tomato paste, dried thyme, dried rosemary, dried oregano, salt, and black pepper to the skillet. Stir to combine.
7. Cover the skillet and simmer the ratatouille over low heat for about 20-25 minutes, stirring occasionally, until all the vegetables are tender and the flavors have melded together.
8. Taste the ratatouille and adjust the seasoning, if needed, adding more salt and pepper to taste.
9. Remove the skillet from the heat and let the ratatouille cool slightly.
10. Garnish the ratatouille with chopped fresh basil leaves before serving.
11. Serve the ratatouille warm or at room temperature, either as a side dish or as a main course, with crusty bread or cooked rice.

Enjoy this flavorful and comforting French Provençal vegetable stew!

Shakshuka (North African Tomato and Egg Dish)

Ingredients:

- 2 tablespoons olive oil
- 1 onion, diced
- 1 bell pepper, diced
- 2 cloves garlic, minced
- 1 teaspoon ground cumin
- 1 teaspoon paprika
- 1/2 teaspoon ground cayenne pepper (adjust to taste)
- 1 can (14 oz/400g) diced tomatoes
- Salt and black pepper to taste
- 4-6 large eggs
- Fresh parsley or cilantro, chopped, for garnish
- Crumbled feta cheese (optional), for garnish
- Crusty bread or pita, for serving

Instructions:

1. Heat the olive oil in a large skillet or cast-iron pan over medium heat.
2. Add the diced onion and bell pepper to the skillet. Sauté for about 5-7 minutes, until softened.
3. Add the minced garlic, ground cumin, paprika, and ground cayenne pepper to the skillet. Cook for another minute, until fragrant.
4. Pour the diced tomatoes into the skillet, along with their juices. Season with salt and black pepper to taste. Stir to combine.
5. Simmer the tomato and pepper mixture for about 10-15 minutes, until the sauce has thickened slightly.
6. Using a spoon, create small wells in the sauce for the eggs. Crack each egg into a well.
7. Cover the skillet and cook the shakshuka for about 5-7 minutes, or until the egg whites are set but the yolks are still runny, or until the eggs are cooked to your desired level of doneness.
8. Remove the skillet from the heat. Sprinkle chopped fresh parsley or cilantro over the top of the shakshuka. If desired, crumble feta cheese over the top for added flavor.
9. Serve the shakshuka hot, straight from the skillet, with crusty bread or pita for dipping.

Enjoy this flavorful and satisfying North African tomato and egg dish!

Tzatziki (Greek Yogurt and Cucumber Dip)

Ingredients:

- 1 large cucumber, peeled and grated
- 1 1/2 cups Greek yogurt
- 2 cloves garlic, minced
- 2 tablespoons extra virgin olive oil
- 1 tablespoon fresh lemon juice
- 1 tablespoon chopped fresh dill (or mint)
- Salt and black pepper to taste

Instructions:

1. Place the grated cucumber in a fine-mesh strainer set over a bowl. Sprinkle with a little salt and let it sit for about 10-15 minutes to release excess moisture.
2. Squeeze the grated cucumber with your hands or wrap it in a clean kitchen towel and squeeze out as much liquid as possible.
3. In a medium bowl, combine the strained cucumber, Greek yogurt, minced garlic, extra virgin olive oil, lemon juice, and chopped fresh dill. Stir until well combined.
4. Season the tzatziki with salt and black pepper to taste. Adjust the seasoning if needed.
5. Cover the bowl with plastic wrap and refrigerate the tzatziki for at least 1 hour to allow the flavors to meld together.
6. Before serving, taste the tzatziki and adjust the seasoning if needed. You can add more lemon juice, garlic, or herbs according to your preference.
7. Serve the tzatziki chilled, garnished with a drizzle of olive oil and a sprig of fresh dill (or mint), if desired.
8. Enjoy the tzatziki as a dip for pita bread, vegetables, or as a sauce for grilled meats or sandwiches.

This homemade tzatziki is fresh, creamy, and packed with flavor—perfect for any occasion!

Italian Margherita Pizza

Ingredients:

- 1 ball of pizza dough (homemade or store-bought)
- 1/2 cup pizza sauce (homemade or store-bought)
- 8 oz (225g) fresh mozzarella cheese, sliced
- 2-3 Roma tomatoes, thinly sliced
- Fresh basil leaves
- Extra virgin olive oil
- Salt and black pepper to taste
- Cornmeal or flour for dusting

Instructions:

1. Preheat your oven to the highest temperature setting (usually around 500°F/260°C) and place a pizza stone or upside-down baking sheet in the oven to preheat.
2. On a lightly floured surface, roll out the pizza dough into a round shape, about 12 inches (30 cm) in diameter. Alternatively, you can stretch the dough by hand.
3. Transfer the rolled-out dough to a pizza peel or another flat surface that's been lightly dusted with cornmeal or flour to prevent sticking.
4. Spread the pizza sauce evenly over the surface of the dough, leaving a small border around the edges.
5. Arrange the sliced fresh mozzarella cheese evenly over the sauce.
6. Place the thinly sliced tomatoes on top of the cheese.
7. Season the pizza with a pinch of salt and black pepper to taste.
8. Slide the assembled pizza onto the preheated pizza stone or baking sheet in the oven.
9. Bake the pizza in the preheated oven for about 10-12 minutes, or until the crust is golden brown and the cheese is bubbly and melted.
10. Once the pizza is out of the oven, garnish it with fresh basil leaves and drizzle with extra virgin olive oil.
11. Slice the Margherita pizza and serve hot.

Enjoy this classic Italian Margherita pizza with its simple yet delicious flavors!

Falafel with Tahini Sauce

Ingredients:

For the falafel:

- 1 can (15 oz) chickpeas, drained and rinsed
- 1/2 cup chopped onion
- 2 cloves garlic, minced
- 1/4 cup chopped fresh parsley
- 1/4 cup chopped fresh cilantro
- 1 teaspoon ground cumin
- 1 teaspoon ground coriander
- 1/4 teaspoon cayenne pepper (optional)
- Salt and pepper to taste
- 2-4 tablespoons all-purpose flour or chickpea flour
- Oil for frying

For the tahini sauce:

- 1/4 cup tahini paste
- 2 tablespoons lemon juice
- 1 clove garlic, minced
- 2-4 tablespoons water (adjust for desired consistency)
- Salt to taste

Instructions:

1. Make the falafel:
    - In a food processor, combine the chickpeas, onion, garlic, parsley, cilantro, cumin, coriander, cayenne pepper (if using), salt, and pepper. Pulse until the mixture is finely ground but not pureed.
    - Transfer the mixture to a bowl and stir in enough flour to bind the mixture together. Start with 2 tablespoons and add more as needed.

- Shape the mixture into small balls or patties and place them on a baking sheet lined with parchment paper.
- Heat oil in a deep skillet or fryer to 350°F (175°C). Fry the falafel in batches until golden brown and crispy, about 3-4 minutes per batch. Remove with a slotted spoon and drain on paper towels.

2. Make the tahini sauce:
    - In a small bowl, whisk together the tahini paste, lemon juice, minced garlic, and salt.
    - Gradually whisk in water, 1 tablespoon at a time, until the sauce reaches your desired consistency. It should be smooth and pourable but not too thin.
3. Serve:
    - Serve the falafel hot with the tahini sauce drizzled over the top or served on the side for dipping.
    - Falafel can be served in pita bread with lettuce, tomatoes, cucumbers, and pickles for a traditional falafel sandwich, or alongside a salad for a lighter option.

Enjoy your homemade falafel with creamy tahini sauce!

Greek Feta and Olive Tart

Ingredients:

For the crust:

- 1 1/4 cups all-purpose flour
- 1/2 teaspoon salt
- 1/2 cup cold unsalted butter, cut into small cubes
- 3-4 tablespoons ice water

For the filling:

- 4 large eggs
- 1 cup heavy cream
- 1/2 cup crumbled feta cheese
- 1/2 cup chopped Kalamata olives
- 1/4 cup chopped fresh parsley
- 1/4 cup chopped fresh dill
- Salt and pepper to taste
- Optional: 1/4 cup chopped sun-dried tomatoes

Instructions:

1. Make the crust:
    - In a food processor, combine the flour and salt. Add the cold butter cubes and pulse until the mixture resembles coarse crumbs.
    - With the processor running, gradually add the ice water until the dough comes together and forms a ball.
    - Turn the dough out onto a lightly floured surface and shape it into a disk. Wrap it in plastic wrap and refrigerate for at least 30 minutes.
2. Preheat the oven:
    - Preheat your oven to 375°F (190°C). Lightly grease a 9-inch tart pan with a removable bottom.
3. Roll out the crust:

- On a lightly floured surface, roll out the chilled dough into a circle large enough to fit into the tart pan. Carefully transfer the dough to the prepared pan and press it into the bottom and sides. Trim any excess dough from the edges.
4. Prepare the filling:
    - In a mixing bowl, whisk together the eggs and heavy cream until well combined.
    - Stir in the crumbled feta cheese, chopped olives, chopped parsley, chopped dill, salt, pepper, and sun-dried tomatoes (if using).
5. Assemble the tart:
    - Pour the filling mixture into the prepared crust, spreading it out evenly.
6. Bake the tart:
    - Place the tart pan on a baking sheet and transfer it to the preheated oven.
    - Bake for 30-35 minutes, or until the filling is set and the crust is golden brown.
7. Serve:
    - Allow the tart to cool slightly before slicing and serving. It can be served warm or at room temperature.
    - Optionally, garnish with additional fresh herbs before serving.

Enjoy your Greek feta and olive tart as a delightful appetizer, side dish, or light lunch!

Mediterranean Stuffed Peppers

Ingredients:

- 4 large bell peppers, any color
- 1 cup cooked quinoa or couscous
- 1 can (15 oz) chickpeas, drained and rinsed
- 1 cup diced tomatoes (fresh or canned)
- 1/2 cup chopped cucumber
- 1/4 cup chopped Kalamata olives
- 1/4 cup crumbled feta cheese
- 2 tablespoons chopped fresh parsley
- 2 tablespoons chopped fresh mint
- 2 cloves garlic, minced
- 1 teaspoon ground cumin
- 1 teaspoon paprika
- Salt and pepper to taste
- Olive oil for drizzling

Instructions:

1. Preheat the oven:
    - Preheat your oven to 375°F (190°C).
2. Prepare the peppers:
    - Cut the tops off the bell peppers and remove the seeds and membranes from the inside. If necessary, slice a thin piece off the bottom of each pepper so they can stand upright in a baking dish.
3. Prepare the filling:
    - In a large mixing bowl, combine the cooked quinoa or couscous, chickpeas, diced tomatoes, chopped cucumber, Kalamata olives, crumbled feta cheese, chopped parsley, chopped mint, minced garlic, ground cumin, paprika, salt, and pepper. Mix well to combine.
4. Stuff the peppers:
    - Divide the filling evenly among the bell peppers, pressing it down gently to pack it in.
5. Bake the stuffed peppers:

- Place the stuffed peppers upright in a baking dish. Drizzle a little olive oil over the tops.
- Cover the dish with aluminum foil and bake in the preheated oven for 30-35 minutes, or until the peppers are tender.

6. Serve:
    - Once the peppers are cooked through, remove them from the oven and let them cool slightly before serving.
    - Optionally, garnish with additional chopped herbs or a sprinkle of feta cheese before serving.

These Mediterranean stuffed peppers make a delicious and nutritious meal on their own, or you can serve them alongside a salad or crusty bread for a complete Mediterranean-inspired feast. Enjoy!

Italian Minestrone Soup

Ingredients:

- 2 tablespoons olive oil
- 1 large onion, chopped
- 2 cloves garlic, minced
- 2 medium carrots, diced
- 2 celery stalks, diced
- 1 medium zucchini, diced
- 1 cup diced potatoes
- 1 cup chopped green beans
- 1 can (15 oz) diced tomatoes (with juices)
- 6 cups vegetable or chicken broth
- 1 can (15 oz) cannellini beans, drained and rinsed
- 1/2 cup small pasta (such as ditalini or elbow macaroni)
- 2 teaspoons dried Italian herbs (basil, oregano, thyme)
- Salt and pepper to taste
- Grated Parmesan cheese for serving
- Chopped fresh parsley for garnish (optional)

Instructions:

1. Sauté aromatics:
    - Heat the olive oil in a large soup pot over medium heat. Add the chopped onion and cook until softened, about 5 minutes. Add the minced garlic and cook for another minute until fragrant.
2. Add vegetables:
    - Add the diced carrots, celery, zucchini, potatoes, and green beans to the pot. Stir to combine and cook for a few minutes until slightly softened.
3. Simmer with tomatoes and broth:
    - Pour in the diced tomatoes with their juices and the vegetable or chicken broth. Bring the soup to a simmer.
4. Add beans and pasta:
    - Once the soup is simmering, add the cannellini beans and small pasta to the pot. Stir well and let the soup continue to simmer for about 10-15 minutes, or until the vegetables are tender and the pasta is cooked.

5. Season and serve:
    - Stir in the dried Italian herbs and season the soup with salt and pepper to taste. Adjust the seasoning as needed.
    - Ladle the hot soup into bowls and serve topped with grated Parmesan cheese and chopped fresh parsley, if desired.
    - Serve with crusty bread or a side salad for a complete meal.

This Italian minestrone soup is comforting, nutritious, and full of flavor. Enjoy it on its own or as part of a cozy Italian dinner!

Greek Lemon Potatoes

Ingredients:

- 4 large potatoes, peeled and cut into wedges
- 1/3 cup olive oil
- 1/3 cup fresh lemon juice
- 3 cloves garlic, minced
- 1 teaspoon dried oregano
- 1 teaspoon dried thyme
- 1 teaspoon dried rosemary
- Salt and pepper to taste
- 1/2 cup chicken or vegetable broth (optional, for extra moisture)

Instructions:

1. Preheat the oven:
   - Preheat your oven to 400°F (200°C).
2. Prepare the potatoes:
   - Peel the potatoes and cut them into wedges. Rinse them under cold water and pat them dry with a paper towel.
3. Make the marinade:
   - In a large bowl, whisk together the olive oil, lemon juice, minced garlic, dried oregano, dried thyme, dried rosemary, salt, and pepper.
4. Marinate the potatoes:
   - Add the potato wedges to the bowl with the marinade. Toss well to coat the potatoes evenly with the mixture.
5. Arrange in a baking dish:
   - Arrange the marinated potato wedges in a single layer in a baking dish. Make sure they're not overcrowded.
6. Roast the potatoes:
   - Place the baking dish in the preheated oven and roast the potatoes for about 45-50 minutes, or until they are golden brown and crispy on the outside, and tender on the inside. Stir the potatoes halfway through the cooking time to ensure even browning.

- If the potatoes start to dry out during roasting, you can add the chicken or vegetable broth to the baking dish to add moisture and prevent them from sticking.
7. Serve:
    - Once the potatoes are done, remove them from the oven and transfer them to a serving dish.
    - Garnish with fresh herbs, if desired, and serve hot as a delicious side dish.

These Greek lemon potatoes are bursting with flavor and make a perfect accompaniment to grilled meats, roasted vegetables, or as part of a Greek-inspired meal. Enjoy!

Moroccan Chicken Tagine with Preserved Lemons

Ingredients:

- 4 bone-in, skin-on chicken thighs
- 2 tablespoons olive oil
- 1 large onion, finely chopped
- 3 cloves garlic, minced
- 1 teaspoon ground cumin
- 1 teaspoon ground coriander
- 1 teaspoon ground cinnamon
- 1/2 teaspoon ground ginger
- 1/2 teaspoon ground paprika
- 1/4 teaspoon ground turmeric
- Pinch of saffron threads (optional)
- Salt and black pepper to taste
- 1 cup chicken broth
- 1/4 cup chopped fresh cilantro
- 1/4 cup chopped fresh parsley
- 1/4 cup chopped preserved lemons (rind only)
- Olives, for garnish (optional)

Instructions:

1. Preheat the oven:
    - Preheat your oven to 350°F (175°C).
2. Prepare the chicken:
    - Season the chicken thighs generously with salt and black pepper.
3. Brown the chicken:
    - Heat the olive oil in a large oven-safe skillet or tagine over medium-high heat. Add the chicken thighs, skin-side down, and cook until golden brown, about 4-5 minutes per side. Remove the chicken from the skillet and set aside.
4. Cook the aromatics:
    - In the same skillet or tagine, add the chopped onion and cook until softened, about 5 minutes. Add the minced garlic and cook for another minute until fragrant.

5. Add the spices:
   - Stir in the ground cumin, ground coriander, ground cinnamon, ground ginger, ground paprika, ground turmeric, and saffron threads (if using). Cook for 1-2 minutes, stirring constantly, until the spices are fragrant.
6. Deglaze the skillet:
   - Pour the chicken broth into the skillet and scrape up any browned bits from the bottom of the pan with a wooden spoon.
7. Simmer the chicken:
   - Return the browned chicken thighs to the skillet, nestling them into the sauce. Bring the mixture to a simmer.
8. Braise in the oven:
   - Cover the skillet or tagine with a lid or aluminum foil and transfer it to the preheated oven. Braise the chicken for 30-35 minutes, or until the chicken is cooked through and tender.
9. Add preserved lemons and herbs:
   - Remove the skillet from the oven. Stir in the chopped fresh cilantro, chopped fresh parsley, and chopped preserved lemons (rind only).
10. Serve:
    - Serve the Moroccan chicken tagine hot, garnished with olives if desired. It pairs well with couscous, rice, or crusty bread.

Enjoy the rich and aromatic flavors of this Moroccan Chicken Tagine with Preserved Lemons!

Caponata (Sicilian Eggplant Dish)

Ingredients:

- 1 large eggplant, diced into small cubes
- Salt
- Olive oil
- 1 onion, finely chopped
- 2 celery stalks, finely chopped
- 3 cloves garlic, minced
- 1 can (14 oz) diced tomatoes, drained
- 1/4 cup green olives, pitted and sliced
- 2 tablespoons capers, rinsed and drained
- 2 tablespoons red wine vinegar
- 1 tablespoon sugar
- 1/4 cup chopped fresh parsley
- Salt and pepper to taste
- Optional: toasted pine nuts or almonds for garnish
- Optional: raisins or currants for a touch of sweetness

Instructions:

1. Prepare the eggplant:
    - Place the diced eggplant in a colander and sprinkle generously with salt. Let it sit for about 30 minutes to draw out any bitterness. Rinse the eggplant thoroughly and pat dry with paper towels.
2. Sauté the vegetables:
    - In a large skillet or saucepan, heat a few tablespoons of olive oil over medium heat. Add the diced onion and celery, and sauté until softened, about 5-7 minutes. Add the minced garlic and cook for another minute until fragrant.
3. Cook the eggplant:
    - Add more olive oil to the skillet if needed, then add the diced eggplant to the pan. Cook, stirring occasionally, until the eggplant is softened and golden brown, about 10-15 minutes.
4. Add tomatoes and seasonings:
    - Stir in the drained diced tomatoes, sliced olives, capers, red wine vinegar, and sugar. Season with salt and pepper to taste.

5. Simmer:
   - Reduce the heat to low and let the caponata simmer gently for about 15-20 minutes, allowing the flavors to meld together and the sauce to thicken slightly. If the mixture seems too dry, you can add a splash of water or vegetable broth.
6. Finish and garnish:
   - Remove the caponata from the heat and stir in the chopped fresh parsley. Taste and adjust the seasoning as needed.
   - Optionally, garnish the caponata with toasted pine nuts or almonds for added crunch and richness. You can also add a handful of raisins or currants for a touch of sweetness if desired.
7. Serve:
   - Serve the caponata warm or at room temperature as a side dish, appetizer, or even a topping for crusty bread or pasta.

Enjoy the rich and savory flavors of this Sicilian caponata!

Greek Souvlaki with Tzatziki Sauce

Ingredients for Souvlaki:

- 1 lb (450g) boneless chicken breast or pork loin, cut into bite-sized pieces
- 2 tablespoons olive oil
- 2 cloves garlic, minced
- 1 teaspoon dried oregano
- 1 teaspoon dried thyme
- 1 teaspoon dried rosemary
- 1/2 teaspoon paprika
- Salt and pepper to taste
- Juice of 1 lemon
- Wooden skewers, soaked in water for at least 30 minutes

Ingredients for Tzatziki Sauce:

- 1 cup Greek yogurt
- 1/2 cucumber, grated and squeezed to remove excess moisture
- 1 clove garlic, minced
- 1 tablespoon lemon juice
- 1 tablespoon chopped fresh dill (or mint)
- Salt and pepper to taste

Instructions:

1. Marinate the meat:
    - In a bowl, combine the olive oil, minced garlic, dried oregano, dried thyme, dried rosemary, paprika, salt, pepper, and lemon juice. Add the chicken or pork pieces to the bowl and toss to coat evenly. Cover and marinate in the refrigerator for at least 30 minutes, or up to 4 hours.
2. Prepare the tzatziki sauce:
    - In another bowl, combine the Greek yogurt, grated cucumber, minced garlic, lemon juice, chopped fresh dill (or mint), salt, and pepper. Stir well to combine. Taste and adjust seasoning if needed. Cover and refrigerate until ready to serve.

3. Skewer the meat:
   - Preheat your grill or grill pan over medium-high heat.
   - Thread the marinated chicken or pork pieces onto the soaked wooden skewers, leaving a little space between each piece.
4. Grill the souvlaki:
   - Lightly oil the grill grates or grill pan to prevent sticking.
   - Grill the skewers for 8-10 minutes, turning occasionally, until the meat is cooked through and has charred grill marks on all sides.
5. Serve:
   - Remove the souvlaki skewers from the grill and let them rest for a few minutes.
   - Serve the grilled souvlaki hot, accompanied by warm pita bread, sliced tomatoes, onions, and lettuce. Drizzle with tzatziki sauce, and enjoy!

Greek souvlaki with tzatziki sauce is a flavorful and satisfying dish that's perfect for a summer barbecue or a casual dinner with friends and family. Enjoy the taste of Greece!

Mediterranean Baked Fish with Herbs and Lemon

Ingredients:

- 4 fish fillets (such as cod, tilapia, or sea bass)
- Salt and pepper to taste
- 2 tablespoons olive oil
- 2 cloves garlic, minced
- 1 tablespoon chopped fresh parsley
- 1 tablespoon chopped fresh dill
- 1 tablespoon chopped fresh basil
- 1 tablespoon chopped fresh oregano
- Zest of 1 lemon
- Juice of 1 lemon
- Lemon slices for garnish
- Optional: 1/4 cup white wine or fish broth

Instructions:

1. Preheat the oven:
    - Preheat your oven to 400°F (200°C). Lightly grease a baking dish large enough to hold the fish fillets in a single layer.
2. Season the fish:
    - Pat the fish fillets dry with paper towels. Season both sides with salt and pepper to taste.
3. Prepare the herb mixture:
    - In a small bowl, combine the olive oil, minced garlic, chopped fresh parsley, chopped fresh dill, chopped fresh basil, chopped fresh oregano, lemon zest, and lemon juice. Mix well to combine.
4. Coat the fish:
    - Place the seasoned fish fillets in the prepared baking dish. Drizzle the herb mixture evenly over the top of the fillets, making sure they are well coated.
5. Add liquid (optional):
    - If using white wine or fish broth, pour it into the bottom of the baking dish around the fish fillets. This will help keep the fish moist during baking.
6. Bake the fish:

- Bake the fish in the preheated oven for 12-15 minutes, or until the fish is cooked through and flakes easily with a fork. Cooking time may vary depending on the thickness of the fillets.
7. Garnish and serve:
    - Once the fish is done, remove it from the oven. Garnish with lemon slices and additional chopped herbs if desired.
    - Serve the Mediterranean baked fish hot, accompanied by your favorite side dishes such as roasted vegetables, couscous, or a fresh salad.

This Mediterranean Baked Fish with Herbs and Lemon is simple to prepare yet full of vibrant flavors that will transport you to the shores of the Mediterranean. Enjoy the light and healthy goodness!

Italian Risotto with Seafood

Ingredients:

- 1 lb (450g) mixed seafood (such as shrimp, scallops, mussels, and/or squid), cleaned and deveined
- 1 1/2 cups Arborio rice
- 4 cups seafood or vegetable broth
- 1/2 cup dry white wine
- 1 shallot, finely chopped
- 2 cloves garlic, minced
- 2 tablespoons olive oil
- 1/2 cup grated Parmesan cheese
- 2 tablespoons unsalted butter
- 1 tablespoon chopped fresh parsley
- Salt and pepper to taste
- Lemon wedges for serving (optional)

Instructions:

1. Prepare the seafood:
    - If using mussels, scrub the shells under cold water and remove the beards. Discard any mussels with cracked or open shells. If using squid, clean the tubes and slice them into rings. Pat the seafood dry with paper towels and season lightly with salt and pepper.
2. Heat the broth:
    - In a saucepan, heat the seafood or vegetable broth over medium heat until it simmers. Reduce the heat to low and keep the broth warm while you prepare the risotto.
3. Sauté the aromatics:
    - In a large, deep skillet or Dutch oven, heat the olive oil over medium heat. Add the chopped shallot and minced garlic and sauté until softened and fragrant, about 2-3 minutes.
4. Toast the rice:
    - Add the Arborio rice to the skillet and stir to coat it with the oil, shallots, and garlic. Cook for 1-2 minutes, stirring constantly, until the rice grains are lightly toasted.

5. Deglaze with wine:
   - Pour in the dry white wine and stir the rice until the wine is absorbed.
6. Add the broth:
   - Begin adding the warm broth to the skillet, one ladleful at a time, stirring frequently. Allow each addition of broth to be absorbed by the rice before adding more. Continue this process for about 18-20 minutes, or until the rice is creamy and tender but still slightly al dente.
7. Cook the seafood:
   - While the risotto is cooking, prepare the seafood. In a separate skillet, heat a tablespoon of olive oil over medium-high heat. Add the seafood to the skillet and cook until just cooked through, about 2-3 minutes for shrimp and scallops, and until the mussels have opened.
8. Finish the risotto:
   - Once the risotto is cooked to your desired consistency, remove it from the heat. Stir in the grated Parmesan cheese and unsalted butter until melted and creamy. Season with salt and pepper to taste.
9. Combine with seafood:
   - Gently fold the cooked seafood into the risotto, along with any juices from the skillet.
10. Serve:
    - Divide the seafood risotto among serving plates or bowls. Garnish with chopped fresh parsley and serve hot, with lemon wedges on the side if desired.

Enjoy this Italian Risotto with Seafood as a deliciously indulgent meal for special occasions or any day you're craving a taste of Italy!

Turkish Baklava

Ingredients:

For the baklava:

- 1 pound (about 450g) phyllo dough, thawed if frozen
- 1 1/2 cups chopped mixed nuts (such as walnuts, pistachios, and almonds)
- 1 cup unsalted butter, melted

For the syrup:

- 1 cup granulated sugar
- 1 cup water
- 1/2 cup honey
- 1 cinnamon stick
- 3-4 whole cloves
- 1 tablespoon lemon juice
- 1 teaspoon rose water (optional)

Instructions:

1. Prepare the syrup:
    - In a saucepan, combine the sugar, water, honey, cinnamon stick, and whole cloves. Bring the mixture to a boil over medium heat, then reduce the heat and let it simmer for about 10-15 minutes, stirring occasionally, until slightly thickened.
    - Remove the saucepan from the heat and stir in the lemon juice and rose water (if using). Let the syrup cool completely, then discard the cinnamon stick and cloves.
2. Prepare the nuts:
    - In a bowl, combine the chopped mixed nuts.
3. Assemble the baklava:
    - Preheat your oven to 350°F (175°C). Grease a 9x13-inch baking dish.

- Unroll the phyllo dough and cover it with a damp towel to prevent it from drying out. Place one sheet of phyllo dough in the bottom of the prepared baking dish and brush it generously with melted butter. Repeat with 7 more sheets of phyllo dough, brushing each layer with butter.
- Sprinkle a layer of the chopped nuts evenly over the phyllo dough.

4. Continue layering:
   - Place another sheet of phyllo dough over the nuts and brush it with butter. Repeat with 7 more sheets of phyllo dough, brushing each layer with butter. Sprinkle another layer of nuts on top. Repeat this process until all the nuts are used, ending with a top layer of phyllo dough, and brushing the top layer generously with butter.

5. Cut and bake:
   - Use a sharp knife to cut the baklava into diamond or square shapes. Be careful not to press down too hard as you cut, so as not to crush the layers.
   - Bake the baklava in the preheated oven for about 45-50 minutes, or until golden brown and crisp.

6. Pour the syrup:
   - Once the baklava is done baking, remove it from the oven and immediately pour the cooled syrup evenly over the hot baklava, allowing it to soak in.

7. Cool and serve:
   - Let the baklava cool completely in the baking dish before serving. This allows the syrup to fully absorb and the flavors to meld.
   - Once cooled, carefully lift the pieces of baklava out of the baking dish and serve on a platter or individual plates.

Enjoy this sweet and decadent Turkish baklava as a delightful dessert or treat!

Mediterranean Chickpea Salad

Ingredients:

- 2 cans (15 oz each) chickpeas (garbanzo beans), drained and rinsed
- 1 English cucumber, diced
- 1 pint cherry tomatoes, halved
- 1/2 red onion, finely chopped
- 1/4 cup Kalamata olives, pitted and halved
- 1/4 cup crumbled feta cheese
- 1/4 cup chopped fresh parsley
- 1/4 cup chopped fresh mint
- 2 tablespoons extra virgin olive oil
- 2 tablespoons red wine vinegar
- Juice of 1 lemon
- 2 cloves garlic, minced
- 1 teaspoon dried oregano
- Salt and black pepper to taste

Instructions:

1. Prepare the chickpeas:
   - Drain and rinse the chickpeas thoroughly under cold water. Place them in a large mixing bowl.
2. Chop the vegetables:
   - Dice the English cucumber, halve the cherry tomatoes, finely chop the red onion, and halve the Kalamata olives. Add them to the bowl with the chickpeas.
3. Add the herbs and cheese:
   - Crumble the feta cheese and chop the fresh parsley and mint. Add them to the bowl with the other ingredients.
4. Make the dressing:
   - In a small bowl, whisk together the extra virgin olive oil, red wine vinegar, lemon juice, minced garlic, dried oregano, salt, and black pepper until well combined.
5. Assemble the salad:

- Pour the dressing over the chickpea and vegetable mixture in the large mixing bowl. Toss gently to coat all the ingredients evenly with the dressing.
6. Chill and marinate:
    - Cover the bowl with plastic wrap or a lid and refrigerate the salad for at least 30 minutes to allow the flavors to meld and the salad to chill.
7. Serve:
    - Once chilled, give the salad a final toss and adjust the seasoning if needed. Transfer it to a serving dish or individual plates.
    - Optionally, garnish with additional chopped herbs or a sprinkle of crumbled feta cheese before serving.

This Mediterranean Chickpea Salad is perfect as a light and healthy meal on its own, or as a side dish to accompany grilled meats, fish, or sandwiches. Enjoy the burst of Mediterranean flavors!

Greek Lemon Chicken Souvlaki

Ingredients:

- 1 1/2 lbs (about 700g) boneless, skinless chicken breasts, cut into bite-sized pieces
- 1/4 cup olive oil
- 1/4 cup freshly squeezed lemon juice
- 2 cloves garlic, minced
- 1 teaspoon dried oregano
- 1 teaspoon dried thyme
- 1 teaspoon dried rosemary
- 1/2 teaspoon paprika
- Salt and black pepper to taste
- Wooden skewers, soaked in water for at least 30 minutes
- Optional: Greek pita bread, tzatziki sauce, chopped tomatoes, sliced red onions, and lettuce for serving

Instructions:

1. Marinate the chicken:
    - In a large bowl, whisk together the olive oil, lemon juice, minced garlic, dried oregano, dried thyme, dried rosemary, paprika, salt, and black pepper.
    - Add the chicken pieces to the bowl and toss to coat them evenly with the marinade. Cover the bowl and refrigerate for at least 1 hour, or preferably overnight, to allow the flavors to meld.
2. Skewer the chicken:
    - Preheat your grill or grill pan over medium-high heat.
    - Thread the marinated chicken pieces onto the soaked wooden skewers, dividing them evenly among the skewers and leaving a little space between each piece.
3. Grill the souvlaki:
    - Lightly oil the grill grates or grill pan to prevent sticking.
    - Grill the chicken skewers for about 5-7 minutes per side, or until the chicken is cooked through and has nice grill marks on all sides.
4. Serve:

- Once the chicken souvlaki is done, remove it from the grill and let it rest for a few minutes.
- Serve the grilled chicken souvlaki hot, accompanied by Greek pita bread, tzatziki sauce, chopped tomatoes, sliced red onions, and lettuce if desired. You can also serve it with a side of Greek salad or roasted vegetables.

Enjoy this Greek lemon chicken souvlaki as a delicious and satisfying meal that's bursting with Mediterranean flavors!

Italian Bruschetta with Tomato and Basil

Ingredients:

- 4-6 ripe tomatoes, diced
- 1-2 cloves garlic, minced
- 1/4 cup fresh basil leaves, chopped
- 2 tablespoons extra virgin olive oil
- 1 tablespoon balsamic vinegar (optional)
- Salt and black pepper to taste
- 1 baguette or Italian bread loaf, sliced
- Olive oil for brushing
- Optional: Balsamic glaze for drizzling

Instructions:

1. Prepare the tomato topping:
    - In a bowl, combine the diced tomatoes, minced garlic, chopped basil, extra virgin olive oil, and balsamic vinegar (if using). Season with salt and black pepper to taste. Mix well to combine. Let the mixture sit for about 10-15 minutes to allow the flavors to meld.
2. Toast the bread:
    - Preheat your oven to 400°F (200°C). Place the bread slices on a baking sheet in a single layer.
    - Brush each slice of bread lightly with olive oil on both sides.
    - Bake in the preheated oven for about 5-7 minutes, or until the bread is toasted and golden brown. You can also toast the bread slices on a grill or grill pan for added flavor.
3. Assemble the bruschetta:
    - Once the bread slices are toasted, remove them from the oven or grill and let them cool slightly.
    - Spoon the tomato mixture generously onto each slice of toasted bread, allowing some of the juices to soak into the bread.
    - If desired, drizzle a little balsamic glaze over the top of each bruschetta for added sweetness and flavor.
4. Serve:

- Arrange the bruschetta on a platter and serve immediately while the bread is still warm and crispy.

Enjoy this classic Italian bruschetta with tomato and basil as a delicious appetizer or snack. It's perfect for summer gatherings, picnics, or anytime you're craving a taste of Italy!

Moroccan Lamb Tagine with Apricots and Almonds

Ingredients:

- 2 lbs (about 900g) lamb shoulder or leg, trimmed of excess fat and cut into chunks
- 2 tablespoons olive oil
- 1 onion, finely chopped
- 3 cloves garlic, minced
- 1 teaspoon ground ginger
- 1 teaspoon ground cumin
- 1 teaspoon ground cinnamon
- 1/2 teaspoon ground coriander
- 1/2 teaspoon ground turmeric
- Pinch of saffron threads (optional)
- Salt and black pepper to taste
- 2 cups chicken or beef broth
- 1/2 cup dried apricots, halved
- 1/4 cup slivered almonds, toasted
- Fresh cilantro or parsley, chopped, for garnish
- Cooked couscous or rice, for serving

Instructions:

1. Brown the lamb:
    - Heat the olive oil in a large tagine or Dutch oven over medium-high heat. Add the lamb chunks in batches and brown them on all sides. Remove the browned lamb from the tagine and set aside.
2. Sauté the aromatics:
    - In the same tagine or Dutch oven, add the chopped onion and cook until softened, about 5 minutes. Add the minced garlic and cook for another minute until fragrant.
3. Add the spices:
    - Stir in the ground ginger, ground cumin, ground cinnamon, ground coriander, ground turmeric, saffron threads (if using), salt, and black pepper. Cook for 1-2 minutes, stirring constantly, until the spices are fragrant.

4. Simmer with broth:
    - Return the browned lamb to the tagine or Dutch oven. Pour in the chicken or beef broth, making sure the lamb is mostly covered. Bring the mixture to a simmer.
5. Braise the lamb:
    - Cover the tagine or Dutch oven with a lid and reduce the heat to low. Let the lamb simmer gently for 1 1/2 to 2 hours, or until the meat is tender and falls apart easily.
6. Add apricots and almonds:
    - About 30 minutes before the lamb is done, add the dried apricots to the tagine. Stir well to combine. Cover and continue to simmer until the apricots are plump and tender.
7. Toast almonds:
    - While the lamb is finishing cooking, toast the slivered almonds in a dry skillet over medium heat until golden brown and fragrant, about 3-5 minutes. Keep an eye on them to prevent burning.
8. Serve:
    - Once the lamb is tender and the apricots are cooked, remove the tagine or Dutch oven from the heat. Taste and adjust the seasoning if needed.
    - Serve the Moroccan lamb tagine hot, garnished with toasted slivered almonds and chopped fresh cilantro or parsley. Serve with cooked couscous or rice on the side.

Enjoy the rich and aromatic flavors of this Moroccan Lamb Tagine with Apricots and Almonds as a satisfying and memorable meal!

Mediterranean Grilled Shrimp with Garlic and Herbs

Ingredients:

- 1 lb (about 450g) large shrimp, peeled and deveined
- 3 cloves garlic, minced
- 2 tablespoons olive oil
- 1 tablespoon chopped fresh parsley
- 1 tablespoon chopped fresh dill
- 1 tablespoon chopped fresh basil
- 1 tablespoon chopped fresh oregano
- Zest of 1 lemon
- Juice of 1 lemon
- Salt and black pepper to taste
- Wooden skewers, soaked in water for at least 30 minutes

Instructions:

1. Prepare the shrimp:
    - If using wooden skewers, soak them in water for at least 30 minutes to prevent burning on the grill. Pat the shrimp dry with paper towels and place them in a bowl.
2. Make the marinade:
    - In a small bowl, combine the minced garlic, olive oil, chopped fresh parsley, chopped fresh dill, chopped fresh basil, chopped fresh oregano, lemon zest, lemon juice, salt, and black pepper. Mix well to combine.
3. Marinate the shrimp:
    - Pour the marinade over the shrimp in the bowl. Toss to coat the shrimp evenly with the marinade. Cover the bowl and refrigerate for at least 30 minutes to allow the flavors to meld.
4. Skewer the shrimp:
    - Preheat your grill to medium-high heat.
    - Thread the marinated shrimp onto the soaked wooden skewers, dividing them evenly among the skewers and leaving a little space between each shrimp.
5. Grill the shrimp:
    - Lightly oil the grill grates to prevent sticking.

- Place the shrimp skewers on the preheated grill. Grill for about 2-3 minutes per side, or until the shrimp are pink and opaque, and have nice grill marks.
6. Serve:
    - Once the shrimp are done, remove them from the grill and transfer them to a serving platter.
    - Serve the Mediterranean grilled shrimp hot, garnished with additional chopped fresh herbs and lemon wedges on the side.

Enjoy these flavorful Mediterranean Grilled Shrimp with Garlic and Herbs as a delightful appetizer or main dish, perfect for summer gatherings or any occasion!

Spanakopita Stuffed Chicken Breast

Ingredients:

- 4 boneless, skinless chicken breasts
- Salt and black pepper to taste
- 1 tablespoon olive oil
- 2 cloves garlic, minced
- 1 small onion, finely chopped
- 5 cups fresh spinach leaves, chopped
- 1/2 cup crumbled feta cheese
- 1/4 cup chopped fresh dill
- 1/4 cup chopped fresh parsley
- 1/4 cup chopped green onions (scallions)
- 1/4 cup plain breadcrumbs
- 2 tablespoons melted butter or olive oil (for brushing)
- Lemon wedges, for serving

Instructions:

1. Preheat the oven:
    - Preheat your oven to 375°F (190°C).
2. Prepare the chicken breasts:
    - Place each chicken breast between two sheets of plastic wrap or wax paper. Use a meat mallet or rolling pin to pound the chicken breasts to an even thickness, about 1/4 inch thick. Season both sides of the chicken breasts with salt and black pepper.
3. Make the filling:
    - Heat the olive oil in a large skillet over medium heat. Add the minced garlic and chopped onion, and sauté until softened and fragrant, about 3-4 minutes. Add the chopped spinach to the skillet and cook until wilted, about 2-3 minutes. Remove the skillet from the heat and let the spinach mixture cool slightly.
    - In a large bowl, combine the cooked spinach mixture, crumbled feta cheese, chopped fresh dill, chopped fresh parsley, chopped green onions, and breadcrumbs. Mix well to combine.
4. Stuff the chicken breasts:

- Place a spoonful of the spinach and feta filling onto one half of each chicken breast. Fold the other half of the chicken breast over the filling to enclose it, creating a stuffed chicken breast. Use toothpicks to secure the edges if needed.
5. Bake the stuffed chicken breasts:
    - Place the stuffed chicken breasts in a greased baking dish. Brush the tops of the chicken breasts with melted butter or olive oil.
    - Bake in the preheated oven for 25-30 minutes, or until the chicken is cooked through and the internal temperature reaches 165°F (75°C).
6. Serve:
    - Once the stuffed chicken breasts are done baking, remove them from the oven and let them rest for a few minutes before serving.
    - Serve the Spanakopita Stuffed Chicken Breast hot, garnished with additional chopped fresh herbs and lemon wedges on the side.

Enjoy this flavorful and satisfying dish with all the delicious flavors of spanakopita in a chicken breast!

Italian Eggplant Parmesan

Ingredients:

- 2 large eggplants, sliced into 1/4-inch rounds
- Salt
- 2 cups breadcrumbs (you can use Italian seasoned breadcrumbs for extra flavor)
- 1 cup all-purpose flour
- 4 large eggs, beaten
- Olive oil, for frying
- 2 cups marinara sauce (homemade or store-bought)
- 2 cups shredded mozzarella cheese
- 1/2 cup grated Parmesan cheese
- Fresh basil leaves, chopped, for garnish (optional)

Instructions:

1. Prep the eggplant:
    - Place the sliced eggplant rounds in a colander and sprinkle them generously with salt. Let them sit for about 30 minutes to draw out excess moisture and bitterness. Rinse the eggplant slices under cold water and pat them dry with paper towels.
2. Bread the eggplant:
    - Set up a breading station with three shallow dishes. Place the flour in one dish, beaten eggs in another dish, and breadcrumbs in the third dish.
    - Dip each eggplant slice into the flour, shaking off any excess. Then dip it into the beaten eggs, allowing any excess to drip off. Finally, coat it evenly with breadcrumbs, pressing gently to adhere. Repeat with the remaining eggplant slices.
3. Fry the eggplant:
    - In a large skillet, heat enough olive oil to cover the bottom of the skillet over medium-high heat. Once the oil is hot, add the breaded eggplant slices in batches, being careful not to overcrowd the skillet. Cook for 2-3 minutes per side, or until golden brown and crispy. Transfer the cooked eggplant slices to a paper towel-lined plate to drain excess oil.
4. Assemble the Eggplant Parmesan:
    - Preheat your oven to 375°F (190°C).

- Spread a thin layer of marinara sauce on the bottom of a baking dish. Arrange a layer of fried eggplant slices on top of the sauce. Spoon more marinara sauce over the eggplant slices, then sprinkle with shredded mozzarella cheese and grated Parmesan cheese. Repeat the layers until all the ingredients are used, finishing with a layer of cheese on top.
5. Bake:
    - Cover the baking dish with foil and bake in the preheated oven for 25-30 minutes, or until the cheese is melted and bubbly.
6. Serve:
    - Once the Eggplant Parmesan is done baking, remove it from the oven and let it cool slightly before serving. Garnish with chopped fresh basil leaves if desired.
    - Serve hot as a main dish, accompanied by a side of pasta or crusty bread.

Enjoy this comforting and flavorful Italian Eggplant Parmesan as a satisfying meal that's sure to please!

Lebanese Fattoush Salad

Ingredients:

For the salad:

- 2 large pita bread rounds, cut into bite-sized pieces
- 2 tablespoons olive oil
- 4 cups romaine lettuce, chopped
- 1 cup cucumber, diced
- 1 cup tomatoes, diced
- 1/2 cup red bell pepper, diced
- 1/2 cup green bell pepper, diced
- 1/4 cup red onion, thinly sliced
- 1/4 cup radishes, thinly sliced
- 1/4 cup fresh mint leaves, chopped
- 1/4 cup fresh parsley leaves, chopped

For the dressing:

- 1/4 cup extra virgin olive oil
- 2 tablespoons freshly squeezed lemon juice
- 1 teaspoon sumac (optional)
- 1 clove garlic, minced
- Salt and black pepper to taste

Instructions:

1. Toast the pita bread:
    - Preheat your oven to 375°F (190°C).
    - Place the bite-sized pita bread pieces on a baking sheet. Drizzle with olive oil and toss to coat evenly.
    - Bake in the preheated oven for 8-10 minutes, or until the pita bread is golden brown and crispy. Remove from the oven and let it cool.
2. Prepare the vegetables:
    - In a large salad bowl, combine the chopped romaine lettuce, diced cucumber, diced tomatoes, diced red and green bell peppers, thinly sliced

red onion, thinly sliced radishes, chopped mint leaves, and chopped parsley leaves.
3. Make the dressing:
   - In a small bowl, whisk together the extra virgin olive oil, freshly squeezed lemon juice, sumac (if using), minced garlic, salt, and black pepper until well combined.
4. Assemble the salad:
   - Add the toasted pita bread pieces to the salad bowl with the vegetables.
   - Drizzle the dressing over the salad and toss gently to coat all the ingredients evenly with the dressing.
5. Serve:
   - Once the salad is dressed, let it sit for a few minutes to allow the flavors to meld together.
   - Serve the Lebanese Fattoush Salad immediately as a refreshing appetizer or side dish, garnished with additional fresh herbs if desired.

Enjoy this vibrant and flavorful Lebanese Fattoush Salad as a light and healthy addition to any meal!

Greek Spanakopita Dip

Ingredients:

- 10 oz (about 300g) frozen chopped spinach, thawed and drained
- 8 oz (about 225g) cream cheese, softened
- 1/2 cup Greek yogurt
- 1/2 cup crumbled feta cheese
- 1/4 cup grated Parmesan cheese
- 1/4 cup chopped green onions (scallions)
- 2 cloves garlic, minced
- 1 teaspoon dried dill
- 1 teaspoon dried oregano
- 1/2 teaspoon salt
- 1/4 teaspoon black pepper
- Olive oil, for drizzling
- Optional: Chopped fresh parsley or dill, for garnish

Instructions:

1. Preheat the oven:
    - Preheat your oven to 375°F (190°C).
2. Prepare the spinach:
    - Thaw the frozen chopped spinach according to the package instructions. Once thawed, place the spinach in a clean kitchen towel or cheesecloth and squeeze out any excess moisture.
3. Mix the ingredients:
    - In a large mixing bowl, combine the drained spinach, softened cream cheese, Greek yogurt, crumbled feta cheese, grated Parmesan cheese, chopped green onions, minced garlic, dried dill, dried oregano, salt, and black pepper. Mix well until all the ingredients are evenly combined.
4. Bake the dip:
    - Transfer the spinach and cheese mixture to a baking dish or oven-safe skillet, spreading it out evenly.
    - Drizzle a little olive oil over the top of the dip.
    - Bake in the preheated oven for 20-25 minutes, or until the dip is hot and bubbly, and the top is lightly golden brown.
5. Garnish and serve:

- Once the dip is done baking, remove it from the oven and let it cool for a few minutes.
- Garnish with chopped fresh parsley or dill, if desired.
- Serve the Greek Spanakopita Dip warm, with pita bread, crackers, or vegetable sticks for dipping.

Enjoy this creamy and flavorful Greek Spanakopita Dip as a delicious appetizer or snack, perfect for sharing with friends and family!

Moroccan Chickpea and Vegetable Tagine

Ingredients:

- 2 tablespoons olive oil
- 1 onion, diced
- 3 cloves garlic, minced
- 1 teaspoon ground cumin
- 1 teaspoon ground coriander
- 1 teaspoon ground turmeric
- 1/2 teaspoon ground cinnamon
- 1/2 teaspoon ground ginger
- 1/4 teaspoon ground cloves
- 1/4 teaspoon cayenne pepper (optional, for heat)
- 1 can (15 oz) chickpeas, drained and rinsed
- 2 carrots, peeled and diced
- 2 potatoes, peeled and diced
- 1 bell pepper, diced
- 1 zucchini, diced
- 1 can (14 oz) diced tomatoes
- 1 cup vegetable broth
- Salt and black pepper to taste
- Fresh cilantro or parsley, chopped, for garnish
- Cooked couscous or rice, for serving

Instructions:

1. Sauté the aromatics:
    - Heat the olive oil in a large tagine or Dutch oven over medium heat. Add the diced onion and minced garlic, and sauté until softened and fragrant, about 5 minutes.
2. Add the spices:
    - Stir in the ground cumin, ground coriander, ground turmeric, ground cinnamon, ground ginger, ground cloves, and cayenne pepper (if using). Cook for 1-2 minutes, stirring constantly, until the spices are fragrant.
3. Add the vegetables and chickpeas:

- Add the diced carrots, potatoes, bell pepper, zucchini, and drained chickpeas to the tagine or Dutch oven. Stir to coat the vegetables and chickpeas with the spices.
4. Simmer with tomatoes and broth:
    - Pour in the diced tomatoes (with their juices) and vegetable broth. Stir to combine. Bring the mixture to a simmer.
5. Cover and cook:
    - Cover the tagine or Dutch oven with a lid and reduce the heat to low. Let the chickpea and vegetable tagine simmer gently for 25-30 minutes, or until the vegetables are tender and the flavors have melded together. Stir occasionally.
6. Season and garnish:
    - Taste the tagine and season with salt and black pepper to taste, if needed. Stir in chopped fresh cilantro or parsley for added freshness and flavor.
7. Serve:
    - Serve the Moroccan Chickpea and Vegetable Tagine hot, spooned over cooked couscous or rice.
    - Garnish with additional chopped fresh herbs, if desired.

Enjoy this Moroccan-inspired dish as a comforting and nutritious meal, packed with delicious flavors and wholesome ingredients!

Mediterranean Baked Eggplant with Tomatoes and Feta

Ingredients:

- 2 large eggplants
- Salt
- Olive oil, for drizzling
- 2 cloves garlic, minced
- 1 can (14 oz) diced tomatoes, drained
- 1 teaspoon dried oregano
- 1 teaspoon dried basil
- 1/2 teaspoon dried thyme
- 1/4 teaspoon red pepper flakes (optional, for heat)
- Salt and black pepper to taste
- 1/2 cup crumbled feta cheese
- Fresh basil leaves, chopped, for garnish (optional)

Instructions:

1. Preheat the oven:
   - Preheat your oven to 400°F (200°C).
2. Prepare the eggplant:
   - Slice the eggplants into 1/2-inch rounds. Place the eggplant slices on a paper towel-lined baking sheet and sprinkle both sides generously with salt. Let them sit for about 15-20 minutes to release excess moisture.
3. Pat dry and arrange:
   - After the eggplant slices have released moisture, pat them dry with paper towels to remove the excess salt and moisture.
   - Arrange the eggplant slices in a single layer on a baking sheet lined with parchment paper.
4. Prepare the tomato mixture:
   - In a small bowl, mix together the minced garlic, diced tomatoes, dried oregano, dried basil, dried thyme, red pepper flakes (if using), salt, and black pepper.
5. Layer the ingredients:
   - Spoon the tomato mixture evenly over the eggplant slices, spreading it out to cover each slice.

- Crumble the feta cheese over the top of the tomato mixture.
6. Bake:
    - Drizzle a little olive oil over the top of the assembled eggplant slices.
    - Bake in the preheated oven for 25-30 minutes, or until the eggplant is tender and the tomatoes are bubbling and starting to caramelize around the edges.
7. Garnish and serve:
    - Once the Mediterranean Baked Eggplant with Tomatoes and Feta is done baking, remove it from the oven.
    - Garnish with chopped fresh basil leaves, if desired.
    - Serve hot as a delicious side dish or light vegetarian main course.

Enjoy this Mediterranean-inspired dish with its flavorful combination of eggplant, tomatoes, and feta cheese!

Italian Gnocchi with Pesto Sauce

Ingredients:

For the gnocchi:

- 1 lb (about 450g) potato gnocchi (store-bought or homemade)

For the pesto sauce:

- 2 cups fresh basil leaves, packed
- 1/2 cup grated Parmesan cheese
- 1/4 cup pine nuts or walnuts
- 2 cloves garlic, peeled
- 1/2 cup extra virgin olive oil
- Salt and black pepper to taste

Optional toppings:

- Additional grated Parmesan cheese
- Fresh basil leaves
- Cherry tomatoes, halved

Instructions:

1. Prepare the gnocchi:
   - If using store-bought gnocchi, follow the package instructions to cook them in a pot of salted boiling water until they float to the surface, indicating they're done. If using homemade gnocchi, cook them in the same manner until they float.
   - Once cooked, drain the gnocchi and set aside.
2. Make the pesto sauce:
   - In a food processor or blender, combine the fresh basil leaves, grated Parmesan cheese, pine nuts or walnuts, and peeled garlic cloves. Pulse until the ingredients are finely chopped.

- With the food processor running, gradually drizzle in the extra virgin olive oil until the pesto reaches your desired consistency. You may need to scrape down the sides of the bowl occasionally.
- Season the pesto sauce with salt and black pepper to taste. Adjust the seasoning as needed.
3. Combine the gnocchi and pesto:
    - Transfer the cooked gnocchi to a large mixing bowl.
    - Add the freshly made pesto sauce to the gnocchi and toss until the gnocchi are evenly coated with the sauce.
4. Serve:
    - Divide the gnocchi with pesto sauce among serving plates or bowls.
    - Optionally, garnish with additional grated Parmesan cheese, fresh basil leaves, and halved cherry tomatoes.
    - Serve immediately as a delicious main course or side dish.

Enjoy this Italian Gnocchi with Pesto Sauce as a comforting and flavorful meal that's quick and easy to prepare!

Greek Orzo Salad with Feta and Olives

Ingredients:

For the salad:

- 1 1/2 cups orzo pasta
- 1 cucumber, diced
- 1 cup cherry tomatoes, halved
- 1/2 cup Kalamata olives, pitted and halved
- 1/2 cup crumbled feta cheese
- 1/4 cup red onion, thinly sliced
- 1/4 cup fresh parsley, chopped
- 1/4 cup fresh mint leaves, chopped
- Salt and black pepper to taste

For the vinaigrette:

- 1/4 cup extra virgin olive oil
- 2 tablespoons red wine vinegar
- 1 clove garlic, minced
- 1 teaspoon dried oregano
- Salt and black pepper to taste

Instructions:

1. Cook the orzo pasta:
    - In a large pot of boiling salted water, cook the orzo pasta according to the package instructions until al dente. Drain the cooked orzo and rinse it under cold water to stop the cooking process. Set aside to cool.
2. Prepare the vinaigrette:
    - In a small bowl, whisk together the extra virgin olive oil, red wine vinegar, minced garlic, dried oregano, salt, and black pepper to make the vinaigrette. Set aside.
3. Assemble the salad:
    - In a large mixing bowl, combine the cooked and cooled orzo pasta, diced cucumber, halved cherry tomatoes, halved Kalamata olives, crumbled feta

cheese, thinly sliced red onion, chopped fresh parsley, and chopped fresh mint leaves.
- Pour the prepared vinaigrette over the salad ingredients.
- Season with salt and black pepper to taste.
- Toss the salad gently to coat all the ingredients evenly with the vinaigrette.
4. Chill and serve:
    - Cover the Greek Orzo Salad with plastic wrap or a lid and refrigerate it for at least 30 minutes to allow the flavors to meld together.
    - Once chilled, give the salad a final toss and adjust the seasoning if needed.
    - Serve the salad cold as a delicious side dish or light meal.

Enjoy this Greek-inspired Orzo Salad with Feta and Olives as a refreshing and satisfying dish, perfect for picnics, barbecues, or any occasion!

Moroccan Spiced Couscous with Roasted Vegetables

Ingredients:

For the couscous:

- 1 1/2 cups couscous
- 1 1/2 cups vegetable broth or water
- 2 tablespoons olive oil
- 1 teaspoon ground cumin
- 1 teaspoon ground coriander
- 1/2 teaspoon ground cinnamon
- 1/2 teaspoon ground turmeric
- Salt and black pepper to taste

For the roasted vegetables:

- 2 bell peppers (any color), sliced
- 2 zucchini, sliced
- 1 large red onion, sliced
- 1 cup cherry tomatoes
- 3 tablespoons olive oil
- 1 teaspoon ground cumin
- 1 teaspoon ground coriander
- 1/2 teaspoon paprika
- Salt and black pepper to taste

For garnish:

- Fresh cilantro or parsley, chopped
- Lemon wedges

Instructions:

1. Prepare the couscous:

- In a saucepan, bring the vegetable broth or water to a boil. Stir in the couscous, cover the saucepan, and remove it from the heat. Let it sit for 5 minutes.
- Fluff the couscous with a fork to separate the grains.
- In a small bowl, mix together the olive oil, ground cumin, ground coriander, ground cinnamon, ground turmeric, salt, and black pepper. Drizzle this mixture over the cooked couscous and toss to combine. Set aside.

2. Roast the vegetables:
    - Preheat your oven to 400°F (200°C).
    - In a large baking dish, combine the sliced bell peppers, sliced zucchini, sliced red onion, and cherry tomatoes.
    - In a small bowl, whisk together the olive oil, ground cumin, ground coriander, paprika, salt, and black pepper. Drizzle this mixture over the vegetables and toss to coat evenly.
    - Spread the vegetables out in an even layer in the baking dish.
    - Roast in the preheated oven for 25-30 minutes, or until the vegetables are tender and starting to caramelize around the edges.

3. Assemble the dish:
    - Fluff the couscous again with a fork to loosen the grains.
    - Transfer the roasted vegetables to a serving platter and serve alongside the spiced couscous.
    - Garnish with freshly chopped cilantro or parsley and serve with lemon wedges on the side for squeezing over the dish.

Enjoy this Moroccan Spiced Couscous with Roasted Vegetables as a flavorful and nutritious meal!

Mediterranean Grilled Lamb Chops with Mint Sauce

Ingredients:

For the lamb chops:

- 8 lamb chops, about 3/4-inch thick
- 2 cloves garlic, minced
- 2 tablespoons olive oil
- 1 tablespoon lemon juice
- 1 teaspoon dried oregano
- 1 teaspoon dried thyme
- Salt and black pepper to taste

For the mint sauce:

- 1/2 cup fresh mint leaves, chopped
- 2 tablespoons fresh parsley, chopped
- 2 tablespoons red wine vinegar
- 1 tablespoon honey
- 1 clove garlic, minced
- 1/4 cup extra virgin olive oil
- Salt and black pepper to taste

Instructions:

1. Marinate the lamb chops:
   - In a bowl, combine the minced garlic, olive oil, lemon juice, dried oregano, dried thyme, salt, and black pepper. Mix well to create a marinade.
   - Place the lamb chops in a shallow dish and pour the marinade over them, turning to coat evenly. Cover the dish and refrigerate for at least 1 hour, or overnight for best results.
2. Prepare the mint sauce:
   - In a small bowl, combine the chopped fresh mint leaves, chopped parsley, red wine vinegar, honey, minced garlic, extra virgin olive oil, salt, and black

pepper. Stir well to combine. Taste and adjust the seasoning if needed. Set aside.
3. Grill the lamb chops:
    - Preheat your grill to medium-high heat.
    - Remove the lamb chops from the marinade and discard any excess marinade.
    - Grill the lamb chops for 3-4 minutes per side for medium-rare, or longer to your desired level of doneness. The internal temperature should reach 145°F (63°C) for medium-rare or 160°F (71°C) for medium.
    - Once cooked, transfer the lamb chops to a plate and let them rest for a few minutes.
4. Serve:
    - Arrange the grilled lamb chops on a serving platter.
    - Drizzle the mint sauce over the lamb chops or serve it on the side.
    - Garnish with additional fresh mint leaves if desired.
    - Serve the Mediterranean Grilled Lamb Chops with Mint Sauce hot, accompanied by your favorite sides such as roasted vegetables, couscous, or a Greek salad.

Enjoy the succulent flavor of these Mediterranean Grilled Lamb Chops with Mint Sauce, perfect for a special dinner or barbecue gathering!

Italian Panzanella Salad with Tomatoes and Bread

Ingredients:

- 4 cups stale crusty bread, cut into bite-sized cubes
- 4 large ripe tomatoes, chopped
- 1 cucumber, sliced or diced
- 1/2 red onion, thinly sliced
- 1/4 cup Kalamata olives, pitted and halved
- 1/4 cup fresh basil leaves, torn
- 2 tablespoons fresh parsley, chopped
- 2 tablespoons capers, drained
- 2 cloves garlic, minced
- 1/4 cup red wine vinegar
- 1/2 cup extra virgin olive oil
- Salt and black pepper to taste
- Optional: 1/4 cup crumbled feta cheese

Instructions:

1. Prepare the bread:
    - If your bread is not already stale, you can toast the bread cubes in the oven at 350°F (175°C) for about 10-15 minutes until they are dry and crisp. Alternatively, you can leave the bread out overnight to stale.
2. Prepare the dressing:
    - In a small bowl, whisk together the minced garlic, red wine vinegar, and extra virgin olive oil. Season with salt and black pepper to taste. Set aside.
3. Assemble the salad:
    - In a large mixing bowl, combine the stale bread cubes, chopped tomatoes, sliced cucumber, thinly sliced red onion, halved Kalamata olives, torn basil leaves, chopped parsley, and drained capers.
4. Add the dressing:
    - Pour the dressing over the salad ingredients in the bowl. Toss gently to coat all the ingredients evenly with the dressing. Allow the salad to sit for about 10-15 minutes to allow the flavors to meld together and for the bread to soak up some of the dressing.
5. Serve:

- Once the salad is ready, taste and adjust the seasoning if needed.
- If using, sprinkle crumbled feta cheese over the top of the salad just before serving.
- Serve the Italian Panzanella Salad with Tomatoes and Bread as a refreshing appetizer or side dish, perfect for summer gatherings or as part of a Mediterranean-inspired meal.

Enjoy the vibrant flavors and textures of this classic Italian Panzanella Salad with Tomatoes and Bread!

Greek Tzatziki Pasta Salad

Ingredients:

For the tzatziki sauce:

- 1 cup Greek yogurt
- 1/2 English cucumber, grated and squeezed to remove excess moisture
- 2 cloves garlic, minced
- 1 tablespoon lemon juice
- 1 tablespoon extra virgin olive oil
- 1 tablespoon fresh dill, chopped
- Salt and black pepper to taste

For the pasta salad:

- 8 oz (about 225g) pasta (such as fusilli, penne, or rotini)
- 1/2 English cucumber, diced
- 1 cup cherry tomatoes, halved
- 1/4 cup red onion, thinly sliced
- 1/4 cup Kalamata olives, pitted and halved
- 1/4 cup crumbled feta cheese
- 2 tablespoons fresh parsley, chopped
- Salt and black pepper to taste
- Optional: Lemon wedges for serving

Instructions:

1. Prepare the tzatziki sauce:
    - In a bowl, combine the Greek yogurt, grated cucumber, minced garlic, lemon juice, extra virgin olive oil, chopped dill, salt, and black pepper. Mix well until smooth and creamy. Adjust seasoning to taste. Cover and refrigerate until ready to use.
2. Cook the pasta:

- Cook the pasta according to the package instructions until al dente. Drain and rinse under cold water to stop the cooking process. Drain well.

3. Assemble the pasta salad:
    - In a large mixing bowl, combine the cooked and cooled pasta, diced cucumber, halved cherry tomatoes, thinly sliced red onion, halved Kalamata olives, crumbled feta cheese, and chopped parsley.
    - Add the prepared tzatziki sauce to the bowl with the pasta and vegetables. Toss gently to coat all the ingredients evenly with the sauce.
    - Season the pasta salad with salt and black pepper to taste. Adjust seasoning as needed.

4. Chill and serve:
    - Cover the Greek Tzatziki Pasta Salad and refrigerate for at least 30 minutes to allow the flavors to meld together.
    - Once chilled, give the pasta salad a final toss and adjust the seasoning if needed.
    - Serve the Greek Tzatziki Pasta Salad cold, garnished with additional chopped parsley and lemon wedges on the side for squeezing over the salad if desired.

Enjoy this refreshing and flavorful Greek Tzatziki Pasta Salad as a delicious side dish or light meal!

Moroccan Harira Soup

Ingredients:

- 1 cup dried chickpeas, soaked overnight (or canned chickpeas, drained and rinsed)
- 1/2 cup dried lentils (green or brown), rinsed
- 2 tablespoons olive oil
- 1 onion, finely chopped
- 2 cloves garlic, minced
- 2 carrots, diced
- 2 celery stalks, diced
- 1 red bell pepper, diced
- 1 can (14 oz) diced tomatoes
- 6 cups vegetable broth or water
- 1/4 cup chopped fresh cilantro
- 1/4 cup chopped fresh parsley
- 1/4 cup chopped fresh mint
- 1 teaspoon ground turmeric
- 1 teaspoon ground cumin
- 1/2 teaspoon ground cinnamon
- 1/2 teaspoon ground ginger
- 1/4 teaspoon ground black pepper
- Salt to taste
- Juice of 1 lemon
- Optional: Cooked vermicelli noodles or rice for serving

Instructions:

1. Prepare the chickpeas and lentils:
    - If using dried chickpeas, soak them in water overnight. Rinse and drain before using. If using dried lentils, rinse them under cold water.
2. Cook the soup:
    - In a large pot, heat the olive oil over medium heat. Add the chopped onion and minced garlic, and cook until softened and fragrant, about 3-4 minutes.

- Add the diced carrots, celery, and red bell pepper to the pot, and cook for another 5 minutes, stirring occasionally.
- Stir in the ground turmeric, ground cumin, ground cinnamon, ground ginger, ground black pepper, and a pinch of salt. Cook for 1-2 minutes to toast the spices.
- Add the soaked chickpeas (or canned chickpeas) and dried lentils to the pot, along with the diced tomatoes and vegetable broth (or water).
- Bring the soup to a boil, then reduce the heat to low and let it simmer, covered, for about 45-60 minutes, or until the chickpeas and lentils are tender.

3. Add fresh herbs and lemon juice:
    - Once the chickpeas and lentils are cooked, stir in the chopped fresh cilantro, parsley, and mint. Season with salt to taste.
    - Squeeze in the juice of one lemon and stir to combine. Taste and adjust seasoning if needed.
4. Serve:
    - Ladle the Moroccan Harira Soup into bowls. If desired, serve with cooked vermicelli noodles or rice.
    - Garnish with additional fresh herbs before serving.

Enjoy this comforting and nourishing Moroccan Harira Soup, packed with flavor and wholesome ingredients!

Mediterranean Stuffed Zucchini Boats

Ingredients:

- 4 medium zucchinis
- 1 tablespoon olive oil
- 1 onion, diced
- 2 cloves garlic, minced
- 1 bell pepper, diced
- 1 cup cooked quinoa or rice
- 1 cup cherry tomatoes, halved
- 1/2 cup Kalamata olives, pitted and chopped
- 1/4 cup chopped fresh parsley
- 1 teaspoon dried oregano
- 1 teaspoon dried thyme
- Salt and black pepper to taste
- 1/2 cup crumbled feta cheese (optional)
- Lemon wedges for serving

Instructions:

1. Preheat the oven:
    - Preheat your oven to 375°F (190°C).
2. Prepare the zucchinis:
    - Cut the zucchinis in half lengthwise. Using a spoon, scoop out the seeds and flesh from the center of each zucchini half to create a hollow "boat." Leave about 1/4 inch of flesh intact.
    - Place the hollowed-out zucchini halves on a baking sheet lined with parchment paper.
3. Prepare the filling:
    - Heat the olive oil in a large skillet over medium heat. Add the diced onion and cook until softened, about 3-4 minutes.
    - Add the minced garlic and diced bell pepper to the skillet, and cook for another 2-3 minutes, until the vegetables are tender.
    - Stir in the cooked quinoa or rice, halved cherry tomatoes, chopped Kalamata olives, chopped fresh parsley, dried oregano, and dried thyme.

Season with salt and black pepper to taste. Cook for an additional 2-3 minutes to heat through.
4. Assemble and bake:
    - Spoon the filling mixture into the hollowed-out zucchini halves, dividing it evenly among them. Press down gently to pack the filling into each boat.
    - If using, sprinkle crumbled feta cheese over the top of each stuffed zucchini boat.
    - Bake in the preheated oven for 20-25 minutes, or until the zucchini is tender and the filling is heated through.
5. Serve:
    - Once cooked, remove the stuffed zucchini boats from the oven.
    - Serve hot, garnished with additional chopped parsley and lemon wedges on the side for squeezing over the boats.

Enjoy these flavorful and nutritious Mediterranean Stuffed Zucchini Boats as a satisfying vegetarian main course or side dish!

Italian Sausage and Pepper Pasta

Ingredients:

- 12 oz (340g) pasta (such as penne, rigatoni, or fusilli)
- 1 lb (450g) Italian sausage, casings removed
- 2 bell peppers (any color), thinly sliced
- 1 onion, thinly sliced
- 3 cloves garlic, minced
- 1 can (14 oz) diced tomatoes
- 1/2 cup tomato sauce
- 1 teaspoon dried oregano
- 1 teaspoon dried basil
- 1/2 teaspoon red pepper flakes (optional, for heat)
- Salt and black pepper to taste
- Grated Parmesan cheese, for serving
- Fresh basil leaves, chopped, for garnish (optional)

Instructions:

1. Cook the pasta:
    - Bring a large pot of salted water to a boil. Cook the pasta according to the package instructions until al dente. Drain the cooked pasta and set aside.
2. Cook the Italian sausage:
    - In a large skillet or saucepan, cook the Italian sausage over medium heat, breaking it up with a spoon, until browned and cooked through, about 8-10 minutes. Remove the cooked sausage from the skillet and set aside.
3. Sauté the vegetables:
    - In the same skillet, add the sliced bell peppers and onion. Cook for 5-7 minutes, or until the vegetables are softened and starting to caramelize.
    - Add the minced garlic to the skillet and cook for an additional 1-2 minutes, until fragrant.
4. Prepare the sauce:
    - Return the cooked Italian sausage to the skillet with the sautéed vegetables.

- Stir in the diced tomatoes (with their juices), tomato sauce, dried oregano, dried basil, and red pepper flakes (if using). Season with salt and black pepper to taste.
- Bring the sauce to a simmer and let it cook for 5-7 minutes to allow the flavors to meld together.

5. Combine with pasta:
    - Add the cooked pasta to the skillet with the sausage and pepper sauce. Toss gently to coat the pasta evenly with the sauce.
6. Serve:
    - Divide the Italian Sausage and Pepper Pasta among serving plates or bowls.
    - Serve hot, garnished with grated Parmesan cheese and chopped fresh basil leaves, if desired.

Enjoy this delicious and satisfying Italian Sausage and Pepper Pasta as a comforting meal for lunch or dinner!

Greek Spinach and Feta Stuffed Chicken Breast

Ingredients:

- 4 boneless, skinless chicken breasts
- Salt and black pepper to taste
- 2 cups fresh spinach leaves, chopped
- 1/2 cup crumbled feta cheese
- 2 cloves garlic, minced
- 1 tablespoon olive oil
- 1 teaspoon dried oregano
- 1 teaspoon dried basil
- 1/2 teaspoon dried thyme
- 1/4 teaspoon red pepper flakes (optional, for heat)
- Toothpicks or kitchen twine, for securing the chicken

Instructions:

1. Preheat the oven:
    - Preheat your oven to 375°F (190°C).
2. Prepare the chicken breasts:
    - Place each chicken breast between two sheets of plastic wrap or parchment paper. Using a meat mallet or rolling pin, pound the chicken breasts to an even thickness, about 1/4 to 1/2 inch thick.
    - Season both sides of the chicken breasts with salt and black pepper to taste.
3. Make the spinach and feta filling:
    - In a skillet, heat the olive oil over medium heat. Add the minced garlic and cook for 1-2 minutes, until fragrant.
    - Add the chopped spinach to the skillet and cook, stirring occasionally, until wilted, about 2-3 minutes.
    - Remove the skillet from the heat and stir in the crumbled feta cheese, dried oregano, dried basil, dried thyme, and red pepper flakes (if using). Mix well to combine.
4. Stuff the chicken breasts:
    - Spoon the spinach and feta filling evenly onto one side of each chicken breast.

- Fold the other side of the chicken breast over the filling to enclose it. Secure the edges with toothpicks or tie with kitchen twine to hold the filling in place.
5. Cook the stuffed chicken breasts:
    - Place the stuffed chicken breasts in a baking dish sprayed with cooking spray or lined with parchment paper.
    - Bake in the preheated oven for 25-30 minutes, or until the chicken is cooked through and no longer pink in the center.
6. Serve:
    - Once cooked, remove the toothpicks or kitchen twine from the chicken breasts.
    - Serve the Greek Spinach and Feta Stuffed Chicken Breast hot, garnished with additional fresh herbs if desired.

Enjoy this delicious and wholesome dish, packed with Mediterranean flavors!

Moroccan Chicken Pastilla (Pie)

Ingredients:

For the chicken filling:

- 2 tablespoons olive oil
- 1 onion, finely chopped
- 2 cloves garlic, minced
- 1 teaspoon ground ginger
- 1 teaspoon ground cinnamon
- 1 teaspoon ground cumin
- 1/2 teaspoon ground turmeric
- 1/4 teaspoon ground cloves
- 1/4 teaspoon ground nutmeg
- 1 lb (450g) boneless, skinless chicken thighs or breasts, diced
- Salt and black pepper to taste
- 1/4 cup chopped fresh cilantro
- 1/4 cup chopped fresh parsley
- 1/4 cup chopped almonds
- 1/4 cup raisins
- 2 eggs, beaten

For assembling the pie:

- 8 sheets phyllo pastry, thawed if frozen
- 1/4 cup melted butter
- Powdered sugar, for dusting (optional)
- Ground cinnamon, for dusting (optional)

Instructions:

1. Prepare the chicken filling:
    - Heat the olive oil in a large skillet over medium heat. Add the chopped onion and minced garlic, and cook until softened, about 3-4 minutes.

- Add the ground ginger, ground cinnamon, ground cumin, ground turmeric, ground cloves, and ground nutmeg to the skillet. Cook for 1-2 minutes, stirring constantly, until fragrant.
- Add the diced chicken to the skillet, season with salt and black pepper, and cook until browned and cooked through, about 8-10 minutes.
- Stir in the chopped cilantro, chopped parsley, chopped almonds, and raisins. Cook for an additional 2-3 minutes, until the flavors are combined.
- Remove the skillet from the heat and let the chicken filling cool slightly. Once cooled, stir in the beaten eggs.

2. Assemble the pie:
    - Preheat your oven to 375°F (190°C).
    - Brush a 9-inch pie dish or tart pan with melted butter.
    - Lay one sheet of phyllo pastry in the prepared pie dish, allowing the edges to overhang. Brush the pastry sheet with melted butter. Repeat with 7 more sheets of phyllo pastry, brushing each layer with melted butter.
    - Spread the chicken filling evenly over the layered phyllo pastry in the pie dish.
    - Fold the overhanging edges of the phyllo pastry over the filling to cover it completely.
    - Brush the top of the pie with melted butter.
    - Use a sharp knife to score the top of the pie into serving portions.
    - Bake in the preheated oven for 25-30 minutes, or until the phyllo pastry is golden brown and crispy.

3. Serve:
    - Once cooked, remove the Moroccan Chicken Pastilla from the oven and let it cool slightly.
    - Dust the top of the pie with powdered sugar and ground cinnamon, if desired.
    - Slice the pie along the scored lines and serve warm.

Enjoy this Moroccan delicacy, Chicken Pastilla, with its delightful blend of savory and sweet flavors!

Mediterranean Roasted Red Pepper Hummus

Ingredients:

- 1 can (15 oz) chickpeas (garbanzo beans), drained and rinsed
- 1/3 cup tahini (sesame paste)
- 1/4 cup fresh lemon juice
- 2 cloves garlic, minced
- 1/4 cup extra virgin olive oil
- 1/2 cup roasted red peppers (from a jar), drained and patted dry
- 1 teaspoon ground cumin
- 1/2 teaspoon smoked paprika
- Salt to taste
- 2-4 tablespoons water, as needed
- Optional garnishes: extra roasted red peppers, chopped fresh parsley, drizzle of olive oil, sprinkle of paprika

Instructions:

1. Roast the red peppers (optional):
    - If you're using fresh red peppers, you can roast them yourself. Preheat your oven broiler. Place whole red peppers on a baking sheet lined with aluminum foil. Broil the peppers, turning occasionally, until they are charred and blistered on all sides, about 10-15 minutes. Remove the peppers from the oven and let them cool. Once cooled, remove the charred skin, seeds, and stems, and then proceed with the recipe.
2. Prepare the hummus:
    - In a food processor, combine the drained chickpeas, tahini, lemon juice, minced garlic, extra virgin olive oil, roasted red peppers, ground cumin, smoked paprika, and a pinch of salt.
    - Blend the ingredients until smooth and creamy, scraping down the sides of the food processor as needed. If the hummus is too thick, add water, 1 tablespoon at a time, until you reach your desired consistency.
    - Taste the hummus and adjust the seasoning as needed, adding more salt or lemon juice if desired.
3. Serve:
    - Transfer the roasted red pepper hummus to a serving bowl.

- Garnish the hummus with additional roasted red peppers, chopped fresh parsley, a drizzle of olive oil, and a sprinkle of paprika, if desired.
- Serve the Mediterranean Roasted Red Pepper Hummus with pita bread, crackers, sliced vegetables, or use it as a spread for sandwiches or wraps.

Enjoy this flavorful and vibrant Mediterranean Roasted Red Pepper Hummus as a delicious dip or spread for any occasion!

Italian Cannellini Bean Soup with Rosemary

Ingredients:

- 2 tablespoons olive oil
- 1 onion, finely chopped
- 2 carrots, diced
- 2 celery stalks, diced
- 3 cloves garlic, minced
- 2 (15 oz) cans cannellini beans, drained and rinsed
- 4 cups vegetable or chicken broth
- 1 sprig fresh rosemary
- 1 bay leaf
- Salt and black pepper to taste
- Grated Parmesan cheese, for serving (optional)
- Crusty bread, for serving (optional)

Instructions:

1. Sauté the aromatics:
    - Heat the olive oil in a large pot over medium heat. Add the chopped onion, diced carrots, and diced celery to the pot. Cook, stirring occasionally, until the vegetables are softened, about 5-7 minutes.
    - Add the minced garlic to the pot and cook for an additional 1-2 minutes, until fragrant.
2. Add the beans and broth:
    - Add the drained and rinsed cannellini beans to the pot with the sautéed vegetables. Stir to combine.
    - Pour in the vegetable or chicken broth, enough to cover the beans and vegetables.
    - Add the sprig of fresh rosemary and bay leaf to the pot.
    - Season with salt and black pepper to taste.
3. Simmer the soup:
    - Bring the soup to a simmer over medium-low heat. Let it simmer gently for about 20-25 minutes, allowing the flavors to meld together and the vegetables to become tender.
4. Remove the rosemary and bay leaf:

- Once the soup has finished simmering, remove the sprig of rosemary and bay leaf from the pot. Discard them.
5. Blend (optional):
    - If desired, use an immersion blender to partially blend the soup until it reaches your desired consistency. This step is optional and can be adjusted based on your preference for a smoother or chunkier soup.
6. Serve:
    - Ladle the Italian Cannellini Bean Soup into bowls.
    - Garnish each serving with grated Parmesan cheese, if desired.
    - Serve the soup hot, accompanied by crusty bread for dipping.

Enjoy this hearty and flavorful Italian Cannellini Bean Soup with Rosemary as a satisfying meal on a chilly day!

Greek Lemon Garlic Roasted Potatoes

Ingredients:

- 2 pounds (about 1 kg) potatoes, such as Yukon Gold or Russet, cut into wedges or cubes
- 4 cloves garlic, minced
- Zest of 1 lemon
- Juice of 1 lemon
- 1/4 cup extra virgin olive oil
- 1 teaspoon dried oregano
- 1 teaspoon dried thyme
- Salt and black pepper, to taste
- Chopped fresh parsley, for garnish (optional)

Instructions:

1. Preheat the oven: Preheat your oven to 400°F (200°C).
2. Prepare the potatoes: Wash and scrub the potatoes, then cut them into wedges or cubes, depending on your preference. Pat the potatoes dry with a paper towel to remove any excess moisture.
3. Make the marinade: In a small bowl, whisk together the minced garlic, lemon zest, lemon juice, extra virgin olive oil, dried oregano, dried thyme, salt, and black pepper.
4. Coat the potatoes: Place the potato wedges or cubes in a large mixing bowl. Pour the marinade over the potatoes and toss until they are evenly coated.
5. Roast the potatoes: Arrange the coated potatoes in a single layer on a baking sheet lined with parchment paper or aluminum foil. Make sure the potatoes are spread out evenly and not overcrowded on the baking sheet. This will help them roast evenly and become crispy.
6. Bake in the oven: Place the baking sheet in the preheated oven and roast the potatoes for about 30-35 minutes, or until they are golden brown and crispy on the outside, and tender on the inside. You can flip the potatoes halfway through the cooking time to ensure even browning.
7. Garnish and serve: Once the potatoes are done, remove them from the oven and transfer them to a serving dish. Sprinkle with chopped fresh parsley for garnish, if

desired. Serve the Greek Lemon Garlic Roasted Potatoes hot as a delicious side dish alongside your favorite main course.

Enjoy these flavorful and aromatic roasted potatoes with the bright flavors of lemon and garlic, perfect for a Greek-inspired meal!

Moroccan Orange and Olive Salad

Ingredients:

- 4 large navel oranges, peeled and sliced into rounds
- 1/2 cup pitted green olives, sliced
- 1/4 cup red onion, thinly sliced
- 2 tablespoons extra virgin olive oil
- 1 tablespoon fresh lemon juice
- 1 tablespoon orange blossom water (optional)
- Salt and black pepper, to taste
- Fresh mint leaves, chopped, for garnish (optional)

Instructions:

1. Prepare the oranges: Peel the oranges and slice them into rounds or half-moons, depending on your preference. Remove any seeds.
2. Assemble the salad: In a large serving bowl, arrange the orange slices. Scatter the sliced green olives and thinly sliced red onion over the oranges.
3. Make the dressing: In a small bowl, whisk together the extra virgin olive oil, fresh lemon juice, and orange blossom water (if using). Season with salt and black pepper to taste.
4. Dress the salad: Drizzle the dressing over the oranges, olives, and onions in the serving bowl. Gently toss to coat the ingredients evenly with the dressing.
5. Garnish and serve: Garnish the Moroccan Orange and Olive Salad with chopped fresh mint leaves, if desired, for a pop of color and freshness. Serve the salad immediately as a refreshing side dish or appetizer.

Enjoy this Moroccan Orange and Olive Salad as a light and flavorful addition to your meal, perfect for warm weather or anytime you crave a burst of citrusy sweetness with a hint of saltiness!